Love.

Goals.

Money.

Problem Solving.

Marriage.

Success.

Significance.

Knowing God.

As Merrill J. Oster shares the wisdom of life with his young-adult daughter, you, too, will find inspiration and guidance to help you become *a woman of purpose.*

Becoming A

Woman

of

PURPOSE

Merrill J. Oster

Here's Life Publishers

P.O. Box 1576, San Bernardino, CA 92402

First printing, March 1989

Published by
HERE'S LIFE PUBLISHERS, INC.
P. O. Box 1576
San Bernardino, CA 92402

ISBN 0-89840-245-X

For More Information, Write:
L.I.F.E.—P.O. Box A399, Sydney South 2000, Australia
Campus Crusade for Christ of Canada—Box 300, Vancouver, B.C., V6C 2X3, Canada
Campus Crusade for Christ—Pearl Assurance House, 4 Temple Row, Birmingham, B2 5HG, England
Lay Institute for Evangelism—P.O. Box 8786, Auckland 3, New Zealand
Campus Crusade for Christ—P.O. Box 240, Colombo Court Post Office, Singapore 9117
Great Commission Movement of Nigeria—P.O. Box 500, Jos, Plateau State Nigeria, West Africa
Campus Crusade for Christ International—Arrowhead Springs, San Bernardino, CA 92414, U.S.A.

Dedicated to the long line of godly women in your family tree, Leah.

Your mother, Carol, whose love, wise counsel and sacrificial example have shaped our family in many meaningful ways.

Your loving grandmother, Pearl Oster, a great mom and "school mom" whose impact on us and hundreds of her students in rural New Hartford, Iowa, is a living testimony to her life.

And your grandmother, Juanita Dempster, another hard working, compassionate woman who is always ready and willing to serve others.

Also, your great-grandmother, Carrie Smith, the grandma who had a large influence on my value system. Her constant concern and prayers benefit us all.

And, to the memory of your great-grandmothers who have lived as committed Christian women...Laura Seamans, Bessie Oster and Elizabeth Dempster.

Without exception, these women were married to wonderful Christian men. Their families enriched their homes, churches and communities. What a rich heritage!

Congratulations on your graduation day! You have done well. Many nice music, broadcasting and theatrical honors speak eloquently of your accomplishments well beyond the minimum requirement for a college degree in communications.

But even more important to your dad and mom, your personality speaks so well of who you are. You have been obedient, you have a highly-developed value system. You have a tender spirit, a willing attitude and a loving concern for those around you. What more could a parent ask?

That's why this book and the companion, *Father to Son: Becoming a Man of Honor,* written to your brother, are not last-minute lectures from Dad as you step out into the world. They are words of reassurance. They remind you of what your family believes and why. There will be enormous pressure on you to water down your value system, because our society's sense of right and wrong is changing.

My hope is that this book will help you and encourage you to stand for truths that have shaped our family and millions of other Christian families for many generations. May these words of hope and optimism give you strength as you swim against the prevailing tide.

Yes, there is life after college. Your mom and I welcome you into this new world. We're here as coach, friend and counsellor. We wish you God's richest blessings!

Contents

1 Love

The Great Power for Good

*And so I am giving a new commandment to you now —
love each other just as much as I love you. Your strong
love for each other will prove to the world that you are
my disciples.*

(John 13:34-35)

*For though we have never yet seen God, when we love
each other God lives in us and His love within us grows
ever stronger.*

(1 John 4:12)

You were less than two years old when you'd jump
up on my lap to answer my "Leah, do you love me?" You'd
hold your thumb and your forefinger about an inch apart
as if to say, "A little bit." I'd reply, "That's nice." Then, with a
grin you'd hold your two hands about six inches apart and
I would exclaim, "That's better!" Then you'd smile broadly
and stretch your hands a foot apart. I'd raise my voice and
say, "That's terrific." Finally, you'd stretch your little arms as
far as they could go and I'd yell, "That is treeeeemennnn-
ndoussss!" And with that, you'd give me a big hug.

That episode became a ritual, repeated hundreds of
times. It was one unique little way we showed each other
our love.

Love is the most powerful force in the world. Whether

11

in the home, church or marketplace, expressions of love set a tone, establish a climate and build a base for good things to happen. Paul says, "If I gave everything I have to poor people, and if I were burned alive for preaching the Gospel but didn't love others, it would be of no value whatever." (1 Corinthians 13:3) Your highest purpose in life is to propagate true love everywhere you go.

When I think of love, I think of the relationship my parents had with me, the relationship your mom and I share, and the one we share with you and your brother, David. We care for each other so much that when one person hurts, we all hurt. When some obstacle is in your way, we want to move it. We enjoy doing things for each other. We are each willing to make great sacrifices to advance the cause of the other.

As channels of love to people around us, we have an opportunity to live lives of purpose. Here's what Peter said.

"*Most important of all, continue to show deep love for each other, for love makes up for many of your faults. Cheerfully share your home with those who need a meal or a place to stay for the night.*

"*God has given each of you some special abilities; be sure to use them to help each other, passing on to others God's many kinds of blessings. Are you called to preach? Then preach as though God himself were speaking through you. Are you called to help others? Do it with all the strength and energy that God supplies, so that God will be glorified through Jesus Christ — to Him be glory and power forever and ever. Amen.*

"*Dear friends, don't be bewildered or surprised when you go through the fiery trials ahead, for this is no strange, unusual thing that is going to happen to you. Instead, be really glad — because these trials will make you partners with Christ in His suffering, and afterwards you will have the wonderful joy of sharing His glory in that coming day when it will be displayed.*"(1 Peter 4:8-13)

This Scripture presents a picture of love quite unlike

the world's view today.

The world's view of love has an emotional and sexual context. The root of Biblical love is action — showing kindness toward another ... writing a check to help someone in need ... denying ourselves in favor of another person ... giving an encouraging word ... doing something for another. God's view of love is one of solid commitment, not passing emotion. It is a commitment to do something for someone else.

The most beautiful example of love is the Lord Jesus Christ. The ultimate act of love was our Lord's death for us. He gave His life so we might have eternal life. He encourages us to show our love toward others, so they, too, will be attracted by His act of love which secures our eternal destiny. Living a life of love is living a life of purpose!

The greatest barrier to loving others is selfishness. 1 Peter 1:22 says, "Now you can have real love for everyone because your souls have been cleansed from selfishness and hatred when you trusted Christ to save you; so see to it that you do love each other warmly with all your hearts."

The power for this kind of love is not in a rugged, disciplined determination to love. You just can't fake love. The power for unselfish love comes only from Jesus Christ and His indwelling Holy Spirit. Again, from 1 Peter 1:23: "For you have a new life. It was not passed on to you in your parents, for the life they give you will fade away. This new one will last forever for it comes from Christ, God's ever-living message to men."

In that same portion of Scripture, Peter talks about other enemies of love. In Chapter 2, verse 1: "So get rid of your feelings of hatred. Don't just pretend to be good! Be done with dishonesty and jealousy and talking about others behind their back."

In today's workplace, many people attempt to get their "jollies" by tearing other people down so they can look good by comparison. That catty, demeaning kind of talk about others is usually a sign of immaturity or jealousy. Jealousy is an enemy of true love. Jealousy demands for self. Of course, when you see incompetence or dishonesty, you must speak up. There is an appropriate time and place for frank, direct criticism of people where common sense standards of performance are not being met. But gossip is not the appropriate way to raise such issues. An attitude of love seeks to correct the errant behavior for the good of the person and the body of Christ. Gossip only widens the circle of knowledge of errant behavior and is a destroyer of good will.

Evil desires sometimes come clothed in an appearance of love. There are phonies in the world who give you a warm, almost slippery smile or a slap on the back, but in their minds all they want is your favor. They are manipulators. They use people. Don't confuse this kind of fakery with real love. Real love goes beyond smooth words. Real love takes action.

The ultimate sign that we are mature Christians is that we show our love to one another. The apostle John wrote:

"If we love other Christians it proves that we have been delivered from hell and given eternal life. But a person who doesn't have love for others is headed for eternal death. Anyone who hates his Christian brother is really a murderer at heart; and you know that no one wanting to murder has eternal life within. We know what real love is from Christ's example in dying for us. And so we also ought to lay down our lives for our Christian brothers.

"But if someone who is supposed to be a Christian has money enough to live well, and sees a brother in need, and won't help him — how can God's love be within him? Little children, let us stop just saying we love people; let us really love them, and show it by our actions." (1 John 3:14-18)

The most fundamental thing a person can do to effectively show genuine love is to know the all-loving God. He is love. Next, we must truly desire to follow Him obediently. Then He will to guide us through life.

2 Salvation

Finding the Right Path

Don't copy the behavior and customs of this world, but be a new and different person with a fresh newness in all you do and think. Then you will learn from your own experience how His ways will really satisfy you. As God's messenger, I give each of you God's warning: Be honest in your estimate of yourselves, measuring your value by how much faith God has given you.

(Romans 12:2-3)

A global spiritual war is raging around us. On one side the forces of God and His army of Christian believers stage the offensive by sharing the Good News of Jesus Christ. Millions each year join God's army. Their lives change. They have new hope. New purpose. A new source of energy, the Holy Spirit.

On the other side the evil forces of Satan aim to distract us from good. His army of anti-God activity raises its head in many subtle ways. Even America, a nation whose founding principles acknowledge God as Creator, is drifting toward Godlessness.

The battle is fought on many fronts. Internationally, the most obvious anti-God force is Communism. Nationally, humanism is one of the big threats. On the personal level, immorality, cults, drugs and selfishness are all anti-God forces gaining momentum in our society.

What's the answer? Winning the battle with Satan at the local level... in the lives of individuals. When an individual turns from self-centeredness to yielding to the call of Jesus, he wins an eternal victory over sin, death and hell. We are declared personal victors. We win the battle, and are recruited to help change the world and to live eternally.

You joined God's army early in life. We were on our way home from a Sunday night gospel meeting. Our good friend and evangelist, Ray Routley, had been the speaker. Since he was staying at our home, he was in the car with us. About halfway between church and home, Ray began to inquire of your brother David, a 7-year-old, where he would spend eternity.

Ray simply and clearly laid out the Gospel message. He pointed out that although we are all born sinners and thereby are unfit to be in the presence of a righteous God, He has prepared a way for us in the person of the Lord Jesus Christ. He explained to David that just as the blood of the Old Testament had been an atonement for man's sin, today the blood of Christ has provided a way of atonement. But, he told David, to become a Christian we must accept this free gift God has provided. He quoted John 3:16, "For God so loved the world that He gave His only begotten son that whosoever believeth in Him should not perish, but have everlasting life." (KJV) Ray didn't press David for a decision. I quietly prayed that David would accept Christ at that moment. But the Spirit didn't move him until two years later.

After we arrived home and had a snack, you and David were sent upstairs to get ready for bed. As was our habit, when you were both ready, one of you yelled down,

"We're ready to pray." After we prayed we usually had a private word with each of you as we tucked you into bed individually. That night as I was about to tuck you in, you said, "Daddy, I want to be saved." I told you to simply believe Jesus Christ died for you and you could be saved. It was a message you had heard many times before — not just earlier in the evening, but in our daily Bible readings and in your Sunday School classes from the time you were old enough to understand the simplest Bible stories. Your response was, "Well, I believe that. Then I'm saved!"

You told your mom the same night, and your grandparents the next day, giving evidence that a real work of the Holy Spirit had, in fact, taken place in your life.

Over the years, by your life and by your words, you have had, and will continue to have, opportunities to point others toward that same truth — Jesus Christ.

God has a plan for each of us. There is a glorious future in view. From the very beginning of time, it has been God's will and God's plan that man should be saved from the penalty of his own sin. The beauty of salvation is that our sins are forgiven, we are put on a new eternal path and we have a personal relationship with God.

Since it is Christ who provides the key to God's plan, it is impossible to get on the right path in life without developing this personal relationship with Jesus Christ. Then we must cultivate a continued state of fellowship with Him and His people. Only by identifying with Him can we hope to share in His victory over death, and thereby share the eternal home He has planned for us.

Although it is important for us to know more and more Biblical truth to mature spiritually, not much else really counts until a person meets the Savior and is indwelt with the power of the Holy Spirit. Then, armed with the

presence and power of the Holy Spirit by having Jesus
Christ living His life through us, we have a sense of direction, an eternal destiny, and assurance of true significance
in life.

You might wonder why I repeat this message which
you have heard from the time you were old enough to
understand. The reason is this: Many pulpits preach messages about God and about Jesus Christ and about important social issues but fail to make salvation by faith a
central theme. As a result, we are a nation where many
people can speak knowledgeably about the Bible but
where relatively few have met the Savior and received the
gift of eternal life personally. The church is becoming
impotent with its watered-down message which ignores
the centrality of salvation by grace.

Salvation and the new birth take place only when an
individual acknowledges his sinfulness, repents, and receives God's gift of eternal life. Call it salvation, being born
again, conversion. By whatever name, it is an act of an
individual's will to submit himself to God, and acknowledge his need of a savior.

I highlight this idea because it is so vitally important. I
hope you hold the doctrine of salvation high as a central
theme when people inquire about why you are different or
ask how you've put your life "all together." By presenting
the simple truths of Scripture, your words can have enormous impact.

I hope you choose a church fellowship which clearly
proclaims the truth of the Gospel message as the only
remedy for man's sin. A local church with sound doctrine,
a good evangelism program and missionary outreach
provides many service and growth opportunities.

It was my good fortune to have two grandmothers
and parents who provided constant reminders that I

needed to know Jesus Christ as Savior. Grandma Bessie Oster took me to Walnut Street Baptist Church in Waterloo, Iowa, whenever Grandma Carrie Smith didn't have me under her wing at the Stout Gospel Hall. Later, when my dad became a Christian, he and Mom, a Christian since her youth, regularly took our family to that little country church in Stout, Iowa.

I knew about "the wages of sin" by the time I was five. But although I listened to Gospel messages intently and memorized Scripture verses at Bible School and Sunday School, I didn't make a personal decision to repent of my sin and acknowledge Christ as my Savior until I was 13 years old.

At 2 a.m. on September 18, 1953, a serious windstorm was brewing. Knowing I wasn't prepared to die, it didn't take much of a wind to send me to the cellar. The rest of the family joined me under the steps — except Dad, who watched the storm from the kitchen window. I was sitting on a 5-gallon bucket. Grandma Carrie was on a chair beside me.

Grandma quoted Acts 16:31, "Believe on the Lord Jesus Christ and thou shalt be saved." At that moment, the simplicity of the Gospel message struck me with new impact. I just believed it. It was no great emotional experience, just simple belief in Christ's finished work at the cross as the complete payment for my sin. I accepted the gift of eternal life. That night under the basement steps, I joined a long line of Christians who have passed this message from one generation to another since the time of Christ. I became a new Christian.

I dashed up the steps and told Dad of my new commitment. The storm subsided. We returned to our beds. The next day I began telling my friends at school. A junior high friend and fellow farm boy, Jim Sluiter, was the first person outside our family to know of my decision. (Five or six years later, he, too, accepted Christ.) I've been telling folks about Christ ever since!

I regularly remind people around me in the workplace that a right relation with Christ is important to me and has practical implications. The message of God's answer to man's sin is too important not to share with friends! A business associate recently testified to others in an office Bible study that he had grown up in a church, lived a moral life, understood an enormous amount about the Bible, about God, and about the life of Jesus Christ. But he didn't personalize his relationship with Christ until after one of our staff conferences. One of us had pointed out the need to make a personal commitment, through an act of our own will.

He said, "I knew all about God, but didn't know Him personally as Savior." Today, he and his wife are trainers for the "evangelism explosion" program in one of the largest churches in our community. He is a humble, quiet-spirited man who consistently allows his young faith to show in many ways in his daily life. Maybe my little light shed some light on his path. Now he is shining his to help others find the right path.

I am confident God will continue to use you as a vessel to steer others to the right path. You already have been an encourager to people around you. Trust God to lead you to daily opportunities to advance His message.

On the subject of the daily walk, Phillip Keller in his book, *Salt For Society*, says, "It is the meek person who finds that faith in God begins to flourish in his life. The self-made, self-sufficient individual sees no need to trust another, let alone Christ, as his master. But the man and woman broken to serve Christ come quickly to the place where they trust Him for guidance and supervision and to supply all their needs. Once on the path, our next step is to trust Him in every area of our lives."

"When you obey me you are living in my love, just as I obey my Father and live in his love." (John 15:10)

3   Obedience

God Tugs. Will You Follow?

And how can we be sure that we belong to Him? By looking within ourselves: are we really trying to do what He wants us to?

(1 John 2:3)

Praise the Lord! For all who fear God and trust Him are blessed beyond expression. Yes, happy is the man who delights in doing His commands.

(Psalm 112:1)

One of the most compelling sights on a farm with horses is watching a young colt. One moment the colt lies flat on its side with its head fully extended, sound asleep, looking lifeless. In a flash, the colt wobbles to its feet, shakes itself, nourishes itself with some mother's milk, then races across the pasture, slowing down only for intermittent periods of raring up first on its front feet, then on its hind feet. At times, the lively animal appears to be totally suspended in midair as it frolics with undisciplined joy.

What a challenge to teach these young horses to be led with a halter and rope! The first time we put a halter on Lightning, your Shetland colt, we learned a lesson in discipline. I tugged at the rope. You and David pushed on

the rump of this stubborn little beast. Lightning planted all
four feet firmly in the sod. The only way we could get him
to move was to twist his head sideways and pull him off
balance so he had to take the first step.

After much tugging and urging, the colt took one or
two steps, then bolted so fast he almost pulled me over as I
struggled to hang onto the end of the lead rope. It took
repeated struggles like that before the colt finally became
"halter-broken." Finally, after many training sessions,
Lightning yielded and followed anywhere you or David
would lead.

Our struggle in becoming "spiritually halter-broken"
is much the same as the colt's until we totally yield to God's
leading. How much easier our lives would be if we would
respond instantly to the gentle tugging of God at our
"halter." However, I have found pride often gets in the way.
At the end of some severe trial in my life, I have found
myself acknowledging to God that I, like the stubborn colt,
had my feet firmly planted as I resisted His will.

It is the disciplined, "halter-broken" person who is
most useful to God. God draws near to the ones who have
"the contrite heart and broken spirit." A humbled spirit is
like a magnet. Other people tend to be drawn close to the
meek person who is transparent, who doesn't take himself
too seriously, who doesn't have to put others down to lift
himself up, and who avoids the pedestal of stubborn self-
importance.

A person who is meek in the spiritual sense is not
timid or weak. The warmth and approachability of a meek
person makes him attractive. The disciplined meek are
not so intently driven and so bent on achieving their own
ends that they fail to take advantage of the opportunities
that come in giving of self to others.

In today's society, where the score is kept by achiev-

ing, attaining, and acquiring, our energies are frequently
misdirected as we get caught up in this sometimes mean-
ingless pursuit. Rather than enjoying our labors of love in
serving others, our activities become burdens to endure
as we view life from the world's self-seeking, "I did it my
way" point of view.

The attitude of the meek is one of being satisfied in
God's service. It is an attitude of using whatever talents,
energy, and abilities God gives us to help other people.
The disciplined, meek person sees no need to impress
others, only to quietly serve them. His main concern is to
advance the cause of Jesus Christ and His kingdom.

To the extent that we obey God's commands and His
specific direction from day to day, His life becomes our life.
His wishes become our wishes. His work becomes ours.
We need to continually remind ourselves of these attributes of the person who is truly successful from God's
point of view.

Our Lord's call is, "Follow me and I will make you
fishers of men." A. W. Tozer in his book, *The Pursuit of God*,
says, "God formed us for His pleasure and so formed us
that we, as well as He, can in divine communion enjoy the
sweet and mysterious mingling of kindred personalities.
He meant us to see Him and live with Him and draw life
from His smile. But we have been guilty of that 'foul revolt'
of which Milton speaks when describing the rebellion of
Satan and his hosts. We have broken with God. We have
ceased to obey Him or love Him and in guilt and fear have
fled as far as possible from His presence."

Tozer points out, "The whole work of God in redemp-
tion is to undo the tragic effects of that foul revolt and bring
us back into a right and eternal relationship with Himself."

Today, the Ten Commandments have been reduced

to the "ten suggestions." We are inundated by a philosophy that says, "You can do it yourself, baby." The world's philosophy of asserting yourself, manipulating your environment, negotiating your way to the top, and demanding your rights, frequently stands in direct opposition to God's purposes.

There are certain personality types, like mine, for whom obedience does not come naturally. I have never been accused of being "Casper Milquetoast." I tend to know where I am going and why, and usually have a clear picture of what I need and how to get it. And I tend to take the shortest possible road, using the least amount of effort, and the fewest words (and sometimes they are not so well chosen).

For this personality type, which tends to be success-oriented, highly driven, and frequently possesses leadership skills, Satan has a special technique. He wants us to gloat and feed on our own successes. He plants in our minds the thought, "The reason for your success is that you are pretty good."

At the point we begin to think of ourselves as basically good, pride takes over and Satan has us set up for a fall. I wish I could not speak with such extensive experience on this issue! There is a message for those who are prone to think they are self-sufficient. Matthew 5:5 reminds us, "Blessed are the meek, for they shall inherit the earth."

The characteristic trait of meekness is one that our society does not understand. The word is used by Jesus in Matthew 11:28-30, "Come unto me all ye that labor and are heavy laden, and I will give you rest. Take my yoke upon you, and learn of me; for I am meek and lowly in heart: and ye shall find rest in your souls. For my yoke is easy and my burden is light."

Phillip Keller in *Salt for Society* points out that the

word meekness "has to do with very tough training, a severe discipline for service, an element of learning to handle heavy loads in the lightest way possible."

Just as those colts on the farm needed to be trained before they could be led, we must train our spirits to come into conformity with the Lord. As in the life of the colt, a period of training brings about a change. Stubborn self-ishness yields to disciplined following whenever the Master tugs. On these words of encouragement, perhaps more than any other in this book, I find the greatest personal struggle.

4 Spiritual Discipline

Staying Fit for the Race

And let us not get tired of doing what is right, for after a while we will reap a harvest of blessing if we don't get discouraged and give up.

(Galatians 6:9)

Don't waste time arguing over foolish ideas and silly myths and legends. Spend your time and energy in the exercise of keeping spiritually fit. Bodily exercise is all right, but spiritual exercise is much more important and is a tonic for all you do. So exercise yourself spiritually and practice being a better Christian, because that will help you not only now in this life, but in the next life too.

(1 Timothy 4:7-8)

It's a windy early-spring March morning. As I look over the back patio, my eyes rest on several hundred acres of Grundy County farmland. Thoughts of your Grandpa Oster flood my mind. About this time of year, he would head to the field to begin careful preparation of the soil.

Even though corn planting time isn't until early May in northern Iowa, the seedbed has to be adequately prepared. Your grandpa didn't plant until soil temperature, soil fertility and soil preparation were just right. Then, even before the crop emerged, he was so anxious to see how his crop was doing that he would dig up the tiny corn seeds to see if they were germinating. He loved to take one of us along to experience the sight of new life breaking through underground. The old corn seed rotted and died as the new little sprout sprung up toward the surface.

By the time the last field of corn was planted in late May, the first field required spraying and cultivation for weeds. The ground, which had already been fertilized earlier, might be fertilized one more time during the growing season. Then there was a waiting period through the summer months before fall harvest.

If any one of the major farming disciplines was left out — or was even late or practiced improperly — it would have a dramatic impact on crop yield. So, your grandpa worked long hours during the early part of the growing season to be sure each detail was completed.

Your grandpa had the reputation of being a good farmer. That meant he practiced all of the disciplines well and consistently had good yields. He was a good steward of the soil. Each year, his standing crops were his proof of a job well done.

There is a spiritual parallel to this stewardship story: stewardship of our "inner garden." The start of the spiritual gardening process is also death. The Lord died that we might have new spiritual life. New life needs cultivation and protection from many elements.

"Bringing order into the spiritual dimension of our private worlds is spiritual gardening," says Gordon McDonald in *Ordering Your Private World*. "The inner garden is a delicate place, and if not properly maintained it will be quickly overrun by intrusive undergrowth. God does not often walk in disordered gardens."

What are the spiritual disciplines that compare with plowing, disking, planting, fertilizing, cultivating, harvesting? Richard Foster in *Celebration of Discipline* lists three categories of disciplines: The inward disciplines are meditation, prayer, fasting and studying. The outward disciplines are simplicity, solitude, submission, and service. The corporate disciplines are confession, worship, guidance and celebration.

I was introduced to Foster's book in a God-planned moment. During the opening minutes of a trustees' meeting at Emmaus Bible College in Dubuque, my fellow trustee, Dick Lauber, shoved a book my way and said, "It's yours, you'll like it." During some slow sections of the board meeting, I read the first few pages of Chapter 1 of *Celebration of Discipline*. I was struck with Foster's opening thoughts, "Superficiality is the curse of our age. The doctrine of instant satisfaction is a primary spiritual problem. The desperate need today is not for a greater number of intelligent people, or gifted people, but for deep people."

Before that trustees' meeting ended, I received an urgent phone call from the chief financial officer of our company. He had uncovered some deep financial problems that required immediate attention. I set up a meeting of our key managers in the family room of our home that night, and began a 2½-year battle for the economic survival of our farming and publishing businesses. Our companies had grown fast, but an economic downturn and trouble with a Chicago lender had thrown us into a very serious situation. We didn't have adequate cash reserves to make it through until harvest.

During the months that followed, I returned to Foster's book and practiced the disciplines of meditation, prayer, fasting and studying. Our management team and many of our employees joined in. The things God did in answer to prayer during this period of difficult months thrills my soul to repeat. I found a Christian financial planner who gave me some good advice. Fellow Christians put together a venture capital-type loan to tide our companies through. We found favor in the eyes of patient creditors. Several specific legal matters that we took to prayer were settled. After a 2½-year struggle, and by the grace of God, we were able to establish ourselves with a bank, the economy began to turn around, and a new satellite-delivered financial services product brought new life to our organization.

All our minds had focused heavily on reorganization. We placed primary management emphasis on two areas of our business, both of which experienced exceptional growth. A combination of cutting costs and increasing revenue resulted in such a dramatic business turnaround that, first as managers, then in a companywide meeting, we acknowledged before everyone that God had worked in a wonderful way in our affairs.

I relate this experience as practical evidence in my own life that when we practice the fundamental disciplines, our spiritual life operates on a higher plane. We communicate more clearly with God, and release enormous spiritual energies to handle our practical everyday problems.

So, my encouragement is to practice the basic disciplines of Christianity the same way athletes practice various disciplines as they prepare to stay in shape for upcoming athletic events.

I had a great lesson in basic discipline in athletics in my high school years. Our New Hartford High School basketball team had won 11 games in a row in 1957. On the night of the 12th game, we apparently were a bit overconfident. We played like undisciplined individuals, not as a team. We fell behind by half time, tried to press too hard in the third quarter and fell even farther behind. Although we rallied a bit in the fourth quarter, we simply couldn't get it together. We lost.

The next day at practice, Coach Jim Spurbeck made us all sit down in the bleachers. He walked back and forth in front of us for a few moments without saying anything. We knew the coach was upset. He really had our attention. Then he ordered, "Oster, get down here!" When I got in front of him, he held out a ball and said, "Oster, *this* is a basketball. Today we're going to practice basketball fundamentals. Now take that ball and see if you can make a layup!" (I had missed three or four the night before.)

For the next two hours we practiced fundamentals of passing, man-to-man defense, blocking out for rebounding, and those basics we had started with in the very early days of fall practice.

We went on to a very good season — ending with an 18-4 record, as I recall. But perhaps the most significant event of the entire season occurred when Coach Spurbeck gave me that lifelong lesson: We frequently need to reapply the fundamentals.

During tough times in our business, our management team returned to both the fundamentals of good business and the fundamentals of our faith.

When we leave the fundamentals, we tend to lead undisciplined spiritual lives. We become tentative. We begin to depend on a value system that is not of God. We lose our eternal perspective on reality, and thereby impair our good judgment.

Perhaps the greatest danger of the undisciplined life is the one highlighted by Gordon McDonald in *Ordering Your Private World*: "Undisciplined spirits lose the fear of accountability to God. There will be growing forgetfulness that all we are and have comes from His good hands, and we will fall into the rut of assuming it is all ours. This happened to Usiah, King of Judah, who had a great relationship with God and then let it lapse (2 Chronicles 26). The result was a growth in pride that led to an embarrassing downfall. He began a hero; he ended the fool. The difference was the growing chaos and disorder in his inner garden."

You have grown up in a Christian home, been through the Sunday School of a good church, attended Christian grade school and high school, and are now about to graduate from Wheaton College. So I won't repeat the basics in detail. I simply remind you there is no substitute for reading the Word and praying regularly as a way of life and heart attitude.

Personally, I know little about the concept of meditation. I couldn't begin to teach it to you. However, in some thoughtful moments during my quiet time while being instructed by the book *Celebration of Discipline*, I have enjoyed wonderful times of fellowship with the Lord. After reading and praying, I sit and wonder at the beauty of His creation from the corner of the room where I normally pray early in the morning. I sometimes feel a sense of God's presence that leads me to answers to my prayer, "God, what should I do about...?"

* * * * * * * * * * * * * * * * * * * *

I just returned from my Saturday afternoon 6-mile run. What a disappointment. I had to work hard to hold an 8-minute average. Just two years ago, I was clipping off country miles at a sub-7-minute pace. As I was chugging up the hill toward home, the striking parallel with spiritual discipline jumped out at me.

If I want to get back to a sub-7-minute mile at long distances, I know exactly what I have to do: a little speed training sprinkled in with consistent distance training. Two years ago, I was running an average of 45 to 55 miles per week. In the last several weeks, I've been making excuses for my undisciplined eating, and have picked up about 15 pounds. Combine that with the fact that I slept in yesterday morning because I said I deserved an extra hour's sleep, and missed my run. As a matter of fact, I used that same excuse two other days this week. That's why my average mileage this winter is under 30 miles per week.

The point is this: I can't successfully improve my running life or my spiritual life by talking about it or by going to meetings about it — I must discipline myself to do it. In training to run, there's no substitute for spending time running. In the spiritual life, there's no substitute for spending time in the presence of God through the disciplines of Bible study and prayer.

Discipline should not result in drudgery if we keep a proper perspective. Foster makes the point that "every discipline has its corresponding freedom. If I have schooled myself in the art of rhetoric, I am free to deliver a moving speech when the occasion requires it. But the moment we make the discipline our central focus, we turn it into law and lose the corresponding freedom.

"The disciplines in themselves are of no value whatever. They have value only as a means of setting us before God so that He can give us the liberation we seek."

I have seen the point Foster is making in my own life from time to time. Sometimes I am so mechanical in the way I read my daily portion of Scripture, and in the way I pray, that I really have not placed myself in the presence of God. I have only fulfilled the "letter of the law" and practiced my discipline. It is much like the half-hearted athlete who goes through all the right motions on the practice field, but whose heart and head are really somewhere else. God wants us — personally and wholeheartedly.

5   Knowing God

Nine Steps in Spiritual Growth

Do you want more and more of God's kindness and peace? Then learn to know him better and better.
(2 Peter 1:2)

Show me the path where I should go, O Lord; point out the right road for me to walk. Lead me; teach me; for you are the God who gives me salvation. I have no hope except in you.
(Psalm 25:4-5)

As a college junior on the Iowa State University campus, I spent one 6-week summer school session without a roommate. I had never experienced loneliness before. Growing up in a busy farm family, with people working close by, I never had a chance to get lonely. My high school and college days were filled with sports, music and leadership activities — always surrounded by people.

But, for six weeks as the only person on the second floor of a rooming house, I was, for the first time in my life, really alone. My college friends had gone home for the summer. The long quiet summer evenings gave opportunity for loneliness to set in. Why didn't I spent the time studying? I can tell you now, academic perfection was not my goal. If I thought I could get a "B" in a class and learn all the fundamentals by listening carefully, reading the book and cramming a little for tests — that was my style. So I had plenty of time on my hands. (I would have a different attitude toward study today.)

That summer, for the first time in my life, I began a serious study of portions of the Bible. I started with the Epistles. Although originally motivated by a desire to "occupy my time," I found that after an hour of reading, studying, taking notes and praying, I felt new energy, a deeper sense of peace and great satisfaction. My hour with the Bible became a regular evening event. My appetite for Bible study grew. Prayer became more important for me. My relationship with the Lord was so meaningful and so uncluttered by interruptions or various demands on my time that I sensed His presence in a way I had never experienced.

Some nights I felt as though the Lord's presence filled the room. My loneliness went away. During that time, I was praying fervently that the Lord would direct me to a Christian woman of His choice and provide means of support. Those prayers were answered in the six months that followed: I renewed my acquaintance with your mom; I received an assistantship at the University of Wisconsin while I got a Master's Degree; I found photography and journalism jobs of such quantity and quality that I was able to leave college with money in the bank after paying for my own education. (To put that in perspective, room, board and tuition were under $2,000 per year. Part-time jobs paid $1.25 to $1.50 per hour, so it was possible to earn my tuition.)

Now let me jump ahead 25 years. The farming and publishing business enterprises we had developed hit tough times in the early 1980's. A crash in land prices undermined our financial underpinnings to such a degree that our largest bank credit line was called by a Chicago lender, even though we had never missed a payment. The lender, pressing hard and fast, had swept up our available cash, then demanded payment of the entire note which we had set up for 3-year repayment. CRISIS!

After calling that prayer and planning meeting of our top executives, I began rising early in the morning to read and pray. Recalling the benchmark experience of my college days, I once again returned to serious reading, study and prayer — after years of sporadic study and half-hearted prayer.

Each morning I would go to the window in the northeast corner of the family room. There between verses my eyes could intermittently gaze over the valley and up into the heavens.

I would pray, read a Psalm, pray, then listen. My mind cleared. My fellowship with the Lord approached that of 25 years earlier. Peace came over me like great waves. The peace came not so much in immediate answer to prayer, but in the knowledge that once again I had yielded control of my life. I prayed. My fellow business associates prayed. Your mom and I prayed together concerning the future.

Over an 18- to 24-month period, we had a list of answered prayer requests so specific and so long that it sends chills down our spines when we praise God for seeing us through those troubled times.

That benchmark experience of knowing God's presence in my early years became my minimum level of expectation through the financial crisis of the early 1980's. Now I have a new benchmark. I find myself frequently going back to the same rocking chair in the same corner of the house for spiritual refreshing, even though I know God is omnipresent and meets me every hour anywhere.

I'm penning these words from that chair.

The desire of my life is to live close to the Lord always. I want to read, pray and meditate in that deep, meaningful way every day. I haven't reached that ideal yet, but I haven't given up. In the meantime, I build on my benchmarks where I have "broken through" to a deeper level of knowing God's presence, of feeling His hand of direction in my life.

I want to encourage you to make a mental marker whenever you enjoy a deeper sense of God's presence, and then build on it. But, don't expect some mystical experience. I believe God promises us direction, peace, counsel, and wisdom when we are obedient and are constantly seeking His leadership. But they never have come to me in "lightening bolts" or "voices." They come in a sense of personal peace, in greater understanding, and in answers to prayer in ways beyond our human reasoning. I am not discrediting those who hear voices, only passing along my personal experience.

I discovered in 2 Peter a logical set of stair steps to success in life. Its base is knowing God.

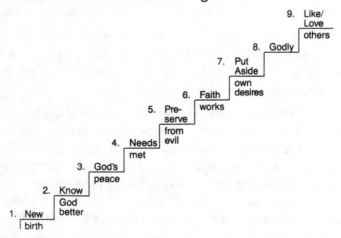

I was glancing through my Bible, reading a portion that I had read many times before. But as the Holy Spirit so often does, He hammered home this portion of Scripture in a new and more powerful way: "Do you want more and more of God's kindness and peace? Then learn to know Him better and better." (2 Peter 1:2) (Since the letter is addressed to Christians, the obvious first step is a step of faith to accept Christ as Savior.)

The step-by-step logic that builds from verse 2 absolutely gripped my soul. The next verse points out that if we get to know Him better, He gives us everything we need. "For as you know Him better, He will give you, through His great power, everything you need for living a truly good life: He even shares His own glory and His own goodness with us" (2 Peter 1:3)

Then He tells us that as we get to know Him better, not only do we get the positives (everything we need), but we are preserved from those negative things that detract from spiritual growth. "And by that same mighty power He has given us all the other rich and wonderful blessings He promised; for instance, the promise to save us from the lust and rottenness all around us, and to give us His own character." (2 Peter 1:4)

To discern God's will, we need a combination of faith and works so we can know what God wants us to do. "But to obtain these gifts, you need more than faith; you must also work hard to be good, and even that is not enough. For then you must learn to know God better and discover what He wants you to do." (2 Peter 1:5) See how closely Scripture ties knowing God with knowing His will in specific decisions in life?

Then, Peter asks us to do something that is very, very difficult — to put aside our own desires. I believe Peter is talking about those selfish desires that are inconsistent with the way God directs us, not the God-given desires that come as a result of obedience. "Next, learn to put aside your own desires so that you will become patient and godly, gladly letting God have His way with you." (2 Peter 1:6)

In verse 7, we find the end result of knowing God. We can begin to enjoy other people more and our love for them grows. "This will make possible the next step, which is for you to enjoy other people and to like them, and finally you will grow to love them deeply." (2 Peter 1:7)

Verse 8 assures us that this step-by-step process gets us on the road to true spiritual growth, on the road to becoming fruitful and useful in the eyes of our Creator. "The more you go on in this way, the more you will grow strong spiritually and become fruitful and useful to our Lord Jesus Christ." (2 Peter 1:8)

In this portion of Scripture we are called to a life of true significance from God's point of view — one of continually seeking to know God more, which results in continually serving Him better by loving others more.

One of the good things about life is that during tough times, when we get in trouble so deep we can't get out without God's help, we seek God and He shows Himself in many new ways. He responds when we show obedience and a sincere desire to know Him better.

6 Ambassadorship

Created With a Purpose

And since I, the Lord and Teacher, have washed your feet, you ought to wash each other's feet.

(John 13:14)

Two years ago on the Wheaton College campus, a freshman student made her way toward the front of the class where a junior was sitting. The freshman looked into the eyes of the junior and said, "You have a certain peace about you that makes me want to know you better. My name is Ann."

What a nice compliment. That's what life is all about. There is no higher or better use in life than to walk in a way in which we attract another person and either point them to Christ or encourage them in their Christian walk.

The exciting part of that campus scene is that the junior girl was you. At that moment, you were experiencing one of the high points in life. This kind of quiet success

goes unannounced to the masses, yet it is surely celebrat-
ed by throngs of angels in the courts of heaven because
you had an impact for eternity.

Even before you were born, your mom and I prayed
that you would grow up to love and serve the Lord and be a
light for others around you. This event was just another
opportunity for us to praise God for answered prayer.

No doubt, that freshman felt estranged and lone-
some. You appeared to be at ease and happy. On that
occasion, you were a channel of blessing. The light of our
Lord Jesus Christ was shining into the life of another
person through you.

Your success in befriending Ann was a bigger event in
God's plan than the winning touchdown scored by a star
running back. It was more significant than getting the lead
role in the college play. When your life became a beacon
for another person, you were front and center in God's
eternal plan. That's living life in the correct lane! Keep
yourself totally available so God can use you as a channel
of blessing. His glory shines through us to provide hope
and direction for others when we are available for service
to Him.

If you ever doubt your value as a person or your
reason for existence, or if you're depressed over feeling
insignificant in a publicity-oriented, show business-type
world, reflect on that classroom experience. You know
through experience God has His hand on you. He wants to
use you for His high and eternal purposes. He will continue using you as long as you make yourself available.

Over the years, other young people have found comfort in your presence. They have shared their dreams and
discussed their troubles because you have presented
them with a servant's attitude. You were available to lend a

hand or an ear.

I hope you cultivate that ability of transparently allowing the light of Jesus Christ to flow to those around you. You are glorifying God with your life when you are a "channel of blessing."

John MacArthur, Jr., in his book, *Keys to Spiritual Growth*, comments, "The supreme objective in the life of any man or woman should be to give God glory. And the great consequence of that goal is unbounded joy! A man does not fulfill his purpose in God's work until he glorifies God, nor does he fulfill his purpose in the personal aspect until he experiences the fullness of joy."

The glory of God is a continuous theme throughout Scripture. As you follow the history of God's glory, that theme focuses on you as a way God reaches people in today's world.

God first revealed His glory in the Garden of Eden to Adam and Eve. This first couple heard the Lord walking in the garden in the cool of the day (Genesis 3:8). After they had sinned, Adam and Eve tried to hide themselves from the presence of the Lord, providing evidence that God came not only in a voice, but in some visible manifestation of His glory. God's glorious attributes were described as a brilliant, shining light, the Shekinah glory — a Hebrew word which means "to dwell" or "reside with".

Because man became rebellious and proud, God's manifested glory was withdrawn from man. Today, God still withdraws himself from those who disobey and arrogantly go their own way.

Next, God's glory shone in the life of one who was both obedient and humble. Moses asked to see God's glory. In Exodus 33:21-23, God told Moses He would give him a glimpse of His glory. The result: A glow made Moses' face shine so radiantly that Aaron and others were afraid to approach him.

The glory of God showed up again in a place called the Tabernacle — a fairly common-looking place because it was made of many weather-beaten animal skins. But, as God so often does, He chose to use this lowly, humble tent as a place to show His glory. However, again man's sin caused God's glory to leave.

Later, God's glory was shown in the Temple (1 Kings 8:10, 11). Here, God in His grace moved down to an earthly level and made His presence known in the lives of His people. But when sin entered the Temple, God's glory departed. When sin enters our lives, we cease to be an effective channel of blessing.

It was a long time before God's glory came back to earth. John 1:14 tells us, "And the word was made flesh, and dwelt among us." His glory returned in the person of the Lord Jesus Christ. The physical evidence of His glory was manifested to the utmost on the Mount of Transfiguration (Luke 9:28-36). In that scene, the three disciples saw for a few minutes all the splendor of His glory. That presence of God's glory was driven away when men condemned Him falsely, nailed Him to a cross, and thereby extinguished history's greatest expression of the glory of God.

But that's not the end of the story! Today, as members of the body of Christ, it is our privilege and responsibility to manifest the glory of God to people around us. One of the many purposes of the body of Christ, the church, is "to give the light of the knowledge of the glory of God in the face of Jesus Christ." (2 Corinthians 4:6)

Once again God has chosen the humble things, humans made from dust, to carry His glory. If the world is ever going to get the message of the Gospel, it is going to get it by seeing God's glory through us. Imagine that! We are temporary "stand-ins" for Jesus Christ himself. What a historic and eternally significant role God gives us during this day of grace!

A person can't begin to give God the glory until he or she comes to Christ. We can begin to give God glory only if we acknowledge Jesus Christ as Savior and Lord. That's why your helping hand to other people should always carry an invitation to know Christ personally. Scripture says, "Yet it was because of this that God raised him up to the heights of Heaven and gave him a name which is above every other name, that at the name of Jesus every knee shall bow in heaven and on earth and under the earth, and every tongue shall confess that Jesus Christ is Lord, to the glory of God the Father." (Philippians 2:9-11)

Many people today seek a success formula. Your quiet, confident spirit, and that special glow God gives those who carry His glory, will attract seekers of truth. "There's something different about you," someone will say. That will be a divine opportunity created by the Holy Spirit, providing a chance for you to present the claims of Jesus Christ to your fellow man.

I know you already freely share the Good News with others. I just want to reaffirm your good work and encourage you to use your smile and your engaging personality in your work place, neighborhood and church to advance the cause of Christ. Kingdom-building is the most important work in life — and the only activity with eternal consequences.

7 Dependence

Nothing Is Too Big for God

*If you want favor with both God and man, and a
reputation for good judgement and common sense,
then trust the Lord completely; don't ever trust yourself.
In everything you do, put God first, and he will direct
you and crown your efforts with success.*
                                                    (Proverbs 3:4-6)

*This I declare, that he alone is my refuge, my place of
safety; he is my God, and I am trusting him.*
                                                    (Psalm 91:2)

Somewhere between Dubuque, Iowa, and Free-
port, Illinois, there is a curve that has an indelible Oster
family memory written on it. We were traveling from our
home in Woodstock, Illinois, back to Iowa to visit relatives
one weekend when you were two years old. Suddenly, you
choked on a piece of candy.

You gasped for breath, began turning blue and sat
there dazed as your mother began to slap you on the back.
I pulled over on the shoulder of that curve, jumped out of
the car and began to use the rescue procedures that I had
learned only weeks before as a member of the Woodstock
rescue squad. However, my best efforts failed. Your eyes
caught mine with an expression that seemed to say, "Can't
you do something, Daddy?"

51

In desperation, your mother did exactly what the rescue squad had taught me not to do. She stuck her finger down your throat and dislodged the piece of candy. You coughed it up and soon your complexion returned from blue to white. What a relief! (A scar on your mom's finger is a lingering reminder of that event.)

In those frightening moments, my only thought was, "Lord, help! Lord, help! Lord, help!" It seems so natural and easy to call on God in a time of crisis.

One of my business associates, the late Pete Fox, had a similar unfortunate experience. One of his friends had a heart attack while the two couples were dining in a restaurant. He told me the story of being absolutely fear-stricken, not knowing what to do. He got his friend, Bill, in a van and began driving as fast as he could towards the hospital. Pete told me his prayer was, "Lord, save Bill. I know it is not too tough for you. After the job you did on Lazarus, Bill should be a piece of cake!" That was a prayer of real faith.

Pete's prayer, his faith and his sense of humor often come back to me, especially when I lack the faith I need to attach to my prayers. How sad and ironic that Pete was killed by a heart attack only two years after his very frightening experience with Bill.

We need to learn to depend on God, not just in crises which we can't control, but in every situation which we think we can control by ourselves.

We so often size up the problem at hand in relationship to our own strength and begin to fear and tremble. That certainly was the situation with the majority of the scouting party described in Numbers 13. They went in to take a look at the promised land. After 40 days, they returned. The majority said the food was great, the land was beautiful, but the cities were well-fortified and there were giants in the land. The crowning statement of the majority of the scouting team in Numbers 13:33 was, "We felt like grasshoppers before them, they were so tall!"

Most of those scouts sized up their problem in relationship to themselves rather than the size of their God. God had already promised them the land. He only asked them to go in and take inventory, not to vote among themselves whether or not they had the personal strength to overcome the giants. As you might expect, a few fearful expressions soon grew into a dominant opinion.

My friend, Pete Fox, on the other hand, sized up Bill's heart attack in relation to bigger problems God had solved in history. That's the kind of dependent attitude God wants.

One of the challenges you face is developing a faith that depends totally upon God. He is able "to do exceedingly abundantly above anything that we ask." A real challenge is to be like Caleb, one of the spies who issued the minority report.

In Numbers 14:7-9, Caleb said, "It is a wonderful country, and the Lord loves us, he will bring us safely into the land and give it to us. It is very fertile, a land flowing with milk and honey! Oh, do not rebel against the Lord, and do not fear the people of the land. For they are but bread for us to eat! The Lord is with us and he has removed his protection from them! Don't be afraid of them!"

The Lord's assessment in Numbers 14:24 sums up the qualities which we need today in a world so filled with self-sufficient people: "Caleb is a different kind of man. He has obeyed me fully. I will bring him into the land he entered as a spy, and his descendants shall have their full share in it." Caleb was a "different" man. He was willing to buck the trend. He went against the current flow of thinking. He was obedient to God.

Whether it be in neighborhood gatherings, or in the business world, or even at the church fellowship, you'll face constant pressure from the world's flow of negative thinking. The majority will attempt to recruit you, or at least to neutralize you. Our world is rapidly polarizing into a majority and minority: Those who stand for and those who stand against basic Biblical principles. In the years ahead, you will need more than human strength to be "different."

The Israelites paid a high price for failing to depend upon God. Numbers 14:25 says, "But now, since the people of Israel are so afraid of the Amalekites and the Canaanites living in the valleys, tomorrow you must turn back into the wilderness in the direction of the Red Sea." All of their generation, except Caleb and Joshua, died in the wilderness.

Many Christians exhibit only enough faith to repent, but they haven't learned obedience, faith and total dependence. Their life is marked with a sense of wandering in the dry, barren wilderness.

The young man who drove me to the airport in Ogallala, Nebraska, this morning asked me what I had been doing in town. I told him I had been teaching a seminar on how to use the Bible as a basis for everyday living and for operating a business.

Without batting an eye, he began telling me about his utter confusion over exactly what to believe. He had grown up in the Catholic Church where he had learned basic facts about faith. He left his parents' church to join a Baptist Church, where he made a profession of faith. Yet, he said, "There are many religions saying so many different things. It's tough to know exactly what to believe."

I assured him that if, in fact, he had repented and

asked the Lord Jesus into his heart, he had taken the right first step. But, that was just one step towards a truly joyful Christian life. Now he had to begin to understand more about the Lord Jesus who died for him and whose Spirit dwells within him.

After we visited, I gave him a booklet from Campus Crusade which summarizes the "Four Spiritual Laws." He acknowledged a real sense of appreciation for my willingness to share with him. He said the chance encounter "made his day." It had made mine, too.

Learning to depend on God is a life-long lesson, but it is greatly aided by simple practices such as showing someone else how to do it. You don't need to be a trained evangelist with all the right words. You don't need hours to explain. God provides the message; we just deliver it.

One of the most exciting telephone calls your mom and I ever received was the evening you called us after a missionary emphasis week at Wheaton. You told us you had rededicated your life to Jesus Christ. When I asked you what you thought had taken place in your life, you said you were going to depend more on Him and less on yourself. You gave every aspect of your life totally to the Lord. All the evidence I can see indicates that you, in fact, deepened your dependence on the Lord. He is answering prayers and taking care of your needs.

Even so, you can expect counterattacks from Satan. He will try to stunt your Christian growth by deceiving you into a "grasshopper" mentality. That thought process trapped the Israelites into thinking they must size up everything in life relative to their own strength. We need to depend on God and size up situations in relation to the power of God and the Holy Spirit. Then we will live truly victorious lives.

8 Goals

Step Your Way Toward Progress

*I strain to reach the end of the race and receive the prize
for which God is calling us up to heaven because of
what Christ Jesus did for us.*

(Philippians 3:14)

*In a race, everyone runs but only one person gets first
prize. So run your race to win. To win the contest you
must deny yourselves many things that would keep you
from doing your best. An athlete goes to all this trouble
just to win a blue ribbon or a silver cup, but we do it for
a heavenly reward that never disappears. So I run
straight to the goal with purpose in every step. I fight to
win. I'm not just shadow-boxing or playing around. Like
an athlete I punish my body, treating it roughly, training
it to do what it should, not what it wants to. Otherwise I
fear that after enlisting others for the race, I myself
might be declared unfit and ordered to stand aside.*

(1 Corinthians 9:24-27)

The crowd at the Cedar Rapids Convention Center
was sitting with great anticipation. The second place winner in the statewide talent competition had just been
announced. Then the master of ceremonies announced,
"First place winner of the talent competition is Leah Jane
Oster of Cedar Falls, Iowa!"

What an exhilarating moment that must have been in

your life! It sure was in mine. Not only were you one of the youngest candidates in the competition, you had swept the judges off their feet with the incredibly difficult "Flight of the Bumblebee."

The next time you're wondering if a goal is unreachable, use past successes (including the many times you walked away with top honors as a pianist) as a reminder that tough things are possible. Let those past successes remind you that the earlier goals were achieved only after lots of planning, prayer and hard work. You can succeed again and again, even as you set more difficult goals, in new areas of life.

You decided you wanted to get into a school that had tough academic standards, even though your high school grades were only a shade above average. Having achieved that goal, you decided to distinguish yourself by being an above-average student. But you weren't satisfied with being only a good student. You decided to tackle extracurricular activities in which you eventually won awards as "outstanding broadcaster of the year" and "outstanding actress of the year," from your peers in campus journalism and theater. These are important benchmarks in your life that should give you a great deal of confidence in tackling a career.

As you step out into the world and begin to size up challenges that seem larger than life, think of some of those major hills you've climbed successfully in the past. The mountains that lie ahead are only a series of slightly steeper hills. But the basics of climbing haven't changed. Set clear-cut goals. Develop checkpoints. Work diligently through the list of specific projects to achieve the big goal. The same basic goal-setting process you have already been through in high school and college will serve you well as you enter the work force, establish a home, and take your place in the community and church.

You are a very fortunate young lady to have already proven in your own life that you can set goals and achieve them with God's help. One of your big challenges in the future will be to properly select those goals which are really worth your time and attention .

Some Christians mistakenly chase the same goals as the rest of the world, only to find after achieving them that they weren't worthwhile. You are a unique person. Your set of goals must be yours. Try not to march to someone else's drumbeat. Through prayer, seek to know God's will for you. Once you have determined God is moving you in a particular direction, goals can help you move in an organized manner.

Goal-setting is critical to making progress in life. If you don't define where you want to go, your life won't be lived with direction and order.

If, over a long period, you feel you aren't achieving any worthwhile goals, you can be a candidate for "burn-out" — a depressing feeling that you are working hard with little to show. Literally millions of people are receiving psychological counsel for depression, deep discouragement and other maladies which might have been averted with a program of steady pursuit of clear cut goals.

Goals are the checkpoints on the journey to a full life. They are the finish lines of our dreams. A clear set of goals gives you an opportunity to check off specific accomplishments as they are completed, giving you a sense of achievement. Without such a list, your failure in one area can unnecessarily pull you down because you fail to give yourself credit for achieving goals in several other areas of your life.

Goals become the criteria for decision making.

Some goals are big and life-long. Paul said in the New Testament, "I press toward the mark of the high calling of God in Christ Jesus." Paul made pleasing God his No. 1 goal. That goal influenced his priorities; it influenced his friendships; it influenced his conversation; and it influenced his attitude toward his captors when he was in prison.

Goals keep us moving in a clearly-stated direction. They give meaning to our lives. Clearly-stated, specific, achievable goals with expected timetables should be reviewed annually in each of these areas of our lives: spiritual, physical, mental, professional, family, personal, social and community.

Perhaps the biggest value of goal setting is keeping a focus on the future, not on the past. Paul said, "Forgetting what is behind and straining toward what is ahead, I press on toward the goal to win the prize for which God has called me heavenward in Christ Jesus." (Philippians 3:13-14)

Goals keep you focused on results. Results are more important than activity. The activity of our lives should be aimed at getting specific results.

Our world is filled with good activities and projects that can absorb all the time you can spare. There is great danger in focusing on activity instead of results. A good way to stop this drift is to take a long, hard look at your goals at the end of a week or a month. Then take a look at the actual record of things which have occupied most of your time that week or month. If the bulk of your activity has been centered on things not related to your goals, you may have to adjust your activity or you will "burn out" in a life of busy but unorganized activity.

The practice of thinking about activity, or hours

invested, in light of goals forces us to become disciplined. Discipline might be defined as clearly understanding our goals, then accomplishing them, regardless of the circumstances. As you crystalize the list of goals in your mind, you find the courage to say "No" to things which clearly don't line up with the direction you believe God is leading you.

Time management is much easier when you keep your goals ever in front of you. Some activities are clearly more important (take higher priority) than others because of your stated goals.

Jesus left us with a good example. He came to do His Father's will. When in Mark 1:32-38 the disciples found Jesus, they said, "Everyone is looking for you." Why wouldn't they be looking for the one who was healing the sick and casting out demons? Jesus replied to the disciples, "Let us go somewhere else, to the nearby villages, so I can preach there also. That is why I have come."

Our Lord could have filled his day with productive activities which would have pleased thousands. But, to accomplish His goal, He had to focus His attention on those activities which would help Him achieve that goal.

"Christian" activities alone are not what God wants from you. First of all, He wants personal fellowship with you. The result of your fellowship with Him should be a desire to carry out His wishes through Christian service.

Paul said something similar to Timothy, "Take pains with these things; be absorbed in them so that your progress (results) might be evident to all." (1 Timothy 4:15) Timothy was not encouraged to *look* spiritual, but to let people see his progress. People would know if he was making mistakes and learning from them.

At the end of this chapter is a form I have revised over

the years, but in one way or another have used at least once a year to redefine what I want to accomplish in life. I remember sitting down with you and your brother David, working through goal-setting when you were in your early teens. I know, in a general way, you have updated your own goals from time to time — at least in your mind.

But I would encourage you to write down specific goals at least once a year and then review them several times during the year. Over a period of years, your achieved goals become important building blocks for greater confidence. As you develop confidence, you are comfortable trying for even bigger goals. You can go back to your goal-setting sheets of five or six years earlier and realize how you are making important progress in specific areas of your life.

Without written benchmarks, sometimes Satan causes us to believe that we are failures — that we have done nothing and that we can do nothing. These feelings of depression are sometimes a result of our estrangement from God, sometimes a result of getting caught up in the way of the world, and sometimes a result of believing Satan's lie.

Continually pray about your goals and ask God's help in achieving them. You will begin to build a line of defense against the depression that Satan sends. Satan wants us to believe that we have no value. Believe me, this is a threat to every human being. We all are threatened by a feeling of insignificance.

Obviously, the best defense against a feeling of insignificance is a sense of understanding who we really are in God's eternal plan for mankind. But a review of your goal sheet gives further verification that not only are you important in God's sight, but He has helped you achieve some specific objectives along the way.

Then, in one form or another, you need to keep a list of things to do. I've changed the format on how I track things to do nearly every year in the last 20 years. One method is to keep a list of short-term, intermediate-term, and longer-range projects. The short-term list might include telephone calls that must be returned, people to see and projects that require your immediate attention. Without constantly reminding yourself of some of the intermediate things and the longer-range things you want to accomplish, your to-do list can become so filled with busy work and activity that you find yourself falling short of achieving your longer-range goals.

This regular reminder that there are longer-range goals in view helps you establish your priorities in the short run. Sometimes you must say "No" to certain activities simply because doing the urgent prevents you from doing the important.

I'm sure this all sounds very mechanical. But writing down specific goals and specific priorities can help you develop an internal discipline that automatically sorts the "urgent" from the important. You then become a disciplined person who shows up on time for appointments and who follows through on all commitments.

When the apostle Paul said, "I press toward the goal," he had in mind a clear-cut set of orders that allowed him to avoid many distractions in life. Those distractions could keep him from achieving his goal of receiving that "Well done, thou good and faithful servant!" when he was called home to be with God.

There is no "right" set of goals for every Christian. God created you as a unique individual. He equipped you with unique spiritual gifts. You have a unique background, unique surroundings and opportunities. You need to consider how you will personally respond to God by developing a lifestyle and life goals that are consistent with the bundle of resources that has been uniquely packaged by God as Leah Jane Oster.

Sometimes it's tempting to march to someone else's tune, to seek the same goals as someone else who appears to be happy and successful. However, true success is in finding God's will in every area of your life, yielding to Him, and moving toward a set of goals that you believe are consistent with God's plan for your life.

Sometimes, to achieve big goals, you have to break them down into small achievable parts. In 1975 as we traveled as a family across western Canada and the U.S. for five weeks, my objective was to expose you to some of the beauties of God's creation in North America. But your mom and I sometimes had to express that goal in terms of how many miles it was to the next swimming pool. On the way between those 30 swimming pools you were able to see the Canadian Rockies, the redwood forest, the desert Southwest, Old Faithful in Yellowstone National Park, and a host of other North American points of interest.

One day you will be a team leader seeking a big goal. To motivate your team, you may have to break the big goal down into smaller, more believable, more easily achievable parts, just as you have done in your personal life.

Here are several good exercises to start your thinking about goal-setting. Ask yourself what you want to contribute, achieve, experience, enjoy and possess in the next five years. Make a list. Take no more than three to five minutes for starters. Then, ask yourself what you want to contribute, achieve, experience, enjoy and possess in the next six months. Again make a list in three to five minutes.

Check those lists out to see which items appear on both. Those are the ones you may want to put at the top of your list and begin working on today.

A second exercise can help you in an even more personal way. Imagine yourself standing around the corner from two people who are talking about you. You hear them. They can't see you. What would you like to hear them say about you? This thought process may bring to mind additional priorities for personal development.

Now, a third exercise to start your thought process on goal-setting. Imagine yourself attending a funeral. Picture the scene vividly in your mind — church, flowers, organ music and all. Now, imagine that the funeral is yours. In the front row are several people waiting to say a brief word about you. One is a friend; another is a person from the church or community; another has worked closely with you; another is a family member. What do you want to hear each of them say? Think about this. Make some notes. These thoughts clarify your goal-setting with a vision of the person you want to be and perhaps the type of things you want to do for others and achieve.

Finally, a fourth exercise. Imagine yourself standing before the Lord Jesus Christ as He is about to show you your rewards for your effort on His behalf on earth. What do you want to hear Him say?

Armed with the notes from these four exercises and a basic inclination on where God is leading your life, you have some raw material for setting your goals for the next year.

9 Good Times

Capture Those God-given Moments

*I bless the holy name of God with all my heart. Yes, I will
bless the Lord and not forget the glorious things he
does for me. He forgives all my sins. He heals me. He
ransoms me from hell. He surrounds me with loving-
kindness and tender mercies. He fills my life with good
things! My youth is renewed like the eagle's!*
(Psalm 103:1-5)

Enroute to achieving some of life's great goals,
develop an ability to enjoy those great, unplanned God-
given moments. If we don't "take time to smell the roses,"
we can miss the real substance of life — an appreciation
for a long list of beautiful moments God gives us.

I suggest you jot down 10 or 15 of these great moments that you've had in life, and remind yourself how
meaningful they are. Then be ready to enjoy some more
like them in the future.

Some of the great moments that provide a sense of
meaning and define "quality of life" for me:
> • An evening around the fireplace with the family.
> • Opening Christmas presents early in the morning.

- A welcome-home hug and kiss from your mom after a day away.

- Sitting on the back patio overlooking the fields watching the shadows lengthen as the sun goes down.

- Listening to the loons on a northern lake at sunset.

- A table filled with family and friends, good food and great conversation.

- Watching a son or a daughter compete or perform.

- Seeing a child reach a milestone such as graduation or marriage.

- Getting together on the hotel room patio watching the sun set over the ocean.

- Enjoying the sound of spring's first birds.

- Hearing water quietly lap against a lakeshore.

- A few minutes around the bed in prayer as a family.

- Rushing to the west kitchen window at someone's urgent request, "Look at that tremendous sunset!"

- Hearing your mom say, "We're going to have a baby!"

- Bringing that baby home and rocking her in my arms.

- Watching that little toddler run across the yard, arms outstretched, wanting to jump into Daddy's arms.

- An evening of casual dining on our patio overlooking the lake.

- Learning something new about history, people or culture in a foreign country — how the Swiss live;

how the New Zealander shears a sheep; how the Hollander trims her windows.

• Watching a child discover new, humorous ways to view the world.

• Reliving through children the excitement of youth, and getting caught up in it and being renewed myself.

• Taking a slow boat cruise up the lake in the early-morning mists.

• Standing in awe at nature's beauty, such as watching Old Faithful erupt, viewing Lake Louise, climbing on a glacier.

• Letting the mud squish between my toes as I walk in the creek.

• Building a tree house with two children handing up the lumber, waiting with great anticipation.

• Being startled by flushing pheasants while walking down a fencerow.

• Getting that smell of autumn that fills the air when the corn leaves turn brown.

• Hearing a "good report" about a friend or acquaintance whom you know is quietly serving God and witnessing with his or her life.

• Listening to another person's problems, and having the joy of watching him or her accept Christ.

• Doing some little favor for someone, then reading a thank-you note.

• Dreaming up an idea, honing it mentally for days, then seeing other people get excited about it, too.
• Watching that idea grow into a product or service,

then later overhearing someone say, "That idea made an enormous difference in my life."

• Hearing a great sermon or beautiful hymn that focuses your thoughts on God.

• Watching a field of soybeans push through a crust of soil, and then change the scenery with their lush green canopy.

• Counting tree rings. Splitting open a corn plant to find the tassel. Watching a seed die to bring forth new life. And being reminded again of the enormous security there is in living in a world that is so intricately and carefully designed by a Creator who loves us so much.

• Sitting on a pail, listening to the rain come down on a tin roof.

• Probing the mind of an outstanding author through the pages of a book.

• Watching the birth of a baby pig, a calf, or a colt, in awe of the instincts of protection and survival placed in those tiny lives.

• Feeling a cool breeze on a warm day.

• Crossing the finish line at the end of a 26.2-mile race.

• Hearing my dad say, "You did a nice job, Son."

• Listening to the roar of the crowd as my free throw bounces around and finally drops through.

• The handshake and hug of a friend I haven't seen for many years.

• A cup of coffee and good conversation with a friend I see every week.

• Watching a mother robin care for a nest of babies.

• Lending an anonymous financial hand to someone in need, then hearing them praise God.

• Reading a missionary's letter, knowing you've had a small part in his or her support.

One of our real challenges in life is to savor these small, rich moments amid the struggle for long-term goals. It's very easy to keep your head down and doggedly pursue some human objective, missing most of God's finest gifts along the way.

ESTIMATE YOUR EXPENSES
PERCENTAGE GUIDE FOR FAMILY INCOME

	$20,000	$30,000	$40,000	$50,000	$60,000	$	%
Gross Income	$20,000	$30,000	$40,000	$50,000	$60,000		
Giving	10%	10%	10%	10%	10%		
Taxes	9.5%	11%	12%	16%	17%		
Social Security	7.15%	7.15%	7.15%	5.7%	4.8%		
Net Spendable	$14,700	$21,500	$28,300	$33,700	$40,400		
Housing	35%	35%	30%	29%	26%		
Food	20%	16%	13%	11%	10%		
Clothing	5%	5%	5%	4%	4%		
Transportation	13%	10%	9%	8%	7%		
Entertainment/ Recreation	6%	7%	7%	8%	8%		
Medical	3%	3%	3%	3%	3%		
Insurance	2%	3%	3%	3%	3%		
Children	3%	2%	2%	2%	2%		
Gifts	2%	2%	2%	2%	2%		
Miscellaneous	5%	5%	5%	5%	5%		
Margin	5%	12%	21%	25%	30%		

ASSUMPTIONS:
1. Figures are based on a family of four.
2. The tax deductions are giving, interest on home mortgage, and state, sales and property taxes (average).
3. Home is owned.
4. There is no debt other than home mortgage.
5. All social security withholdings are from one wage earner.
6. The estimates are based on 1985 tax schedules and allowable deductions.
7. All living expenses are percentages of net spendable income.
8. Margin can be used for other expenses (debt, private education, savings, etc.).

10 Money

Your Checkbook: A "Spiritual Thermometer"

For the love of money is the first step toward all kinds of sin. Some people have even turned away from God because of their love for it, and as a result have pierced themselves with many sorrows.

(1 Timothy 6:10)

But anyone who won't care for his own relatives when they need help, especially those living in his own family, has no right to say he is a Christian. Such a person is worse than the heathen.

(1 Timothy 5:8)

There are two extreme attitudes toward money. On one end of the spectrum you'll see people totally driven towards financial accumulation. They measure every decision in dollars. At the other extreme, there are people who take such a casual attitude toward money that they don't adequately care for their families.

The challenge of the Christian family today is to live somewhere between those two errors, having enough respect for fiscal responsibility to care for our own family, but not such a lust for money that it becomes our god.

Our cultural background has a huge impact on our attitude toward money. Your Grandma Oster tells of a winter in her life during the Great Depression when the

Smith family was so short of money that she walked up and down the railroad tracks picking up pieces of coal which they needed for fuel. Great-Grandma Smith made all of the family's clothes and took in sewing to help make ends meet. They weren't always sure from one day to the next whether they would have anything to eat.

As a result of that background, my parents drilled into me the importance of financial responsibility. I saw it lived out in their lives. They frequently called my attention to people around us who were living irresponsibly and pointed out the results of that waste. So, learning about practical economics was no problem for my generation.

However, that kind of austere upbringing has led many people to seek money as their source of security and power. Eventually, money becomes their only god. Such a life is a vivid definition of emptiness.

I'd like to pass along to you some worthwhile financial principles I've learned from earlier generations of our family.

1. **If you have to work for it, you appreciate it more.** Although this is a generalization that has many exceptions, it is usually true that people who must save money for something over a long period usually have a greater sense of satisfaction when they finally achieve a financial goal. People tend to take better care of an earned property than a gifted property.

Out of that generalization, your mother and I have insisted that you and David earn a significant part of your college education expenses. Even though you are driving an old car that has some rust spots, lots of rattles, and a few little things that don't work, your mother and I have no inclination to buy a new one for you. We don't want to steal the joy that comes from working hard and saving up for your own new car and finally realizing your goal. As I walk through the parking lots on your college campus, it's obvious there are lots of fine parents in this world who do not share that opinion. I'm not about to climb on a soap box and say they're wrong. On the other hand, my experience of working for my own first new car brought a great thrill and satisfaction. Let me share our story:

I walked home from work one noon during the early years of our marriage to announce to your mom that my salary had been increased to $10,000 per year. I said, "Sweetheart, we have it made." I grabbed a Pepsi, we walked out on the patio where I propped my feet up on the edge and leaned back to enjoy this moment of enormous success. I told her, "With the added income, I think it's safe now to use our savings for a new car."

I went to the Ford dealership in Woodstock, Ill., and negotiated the cash price of $2,700 for a 1964 Ford Galaxie. It was a great moment. Whether it's a car, a down payment on your first home, or some other item, I'm eager for you to enjoy the privilege of seeing with your own eyes the fruits of your own labor.

2. **"A penny saved is a penny earned"** or, don't spend it before you get it. Today's typical family is awash on a sea of credit card debt. You may need one or two credit cards for identification purposes and for emergencies. But I'd suggest either never using them for anything else, or using them only to the extent that you're willing to pay your total outstanding balance at the end of every month.

Proverbs tells us, "The borrower becomes the lender's slave." There's such enormous slavery to over-spending in our country today. Money disagreements are the No. 1 reason married couples split up. The debts pile up, they blame each other, and the seeds of marriage disaster have been sown by money.

3. **The formula for wealth: Spend less than you earn and do it for a long time.** This sounds like a very simple principle. Yet I've heard Ron Blue, the author of *Master Your Money*, give this advice in his very sophisticated financial planning seminars. We should never assume that a simple principle is not fundamentally the most important, especially when it comes to money management. There's no substitute for living within your means and saving a little every month. You build a nest egg that will provide financial security.

How much money is enough? When it comes to money, God gives you two things to consider. First, He gives you the financial resources you need. Second, He presents you with the opportunities to share them with others. Abundance and sacrifice. You need to consider both in order to answer the Christian's money question, "How much?" That's the attitude of a money column in *U Magazine* which also made the following four suggestions:

1. Take the time to sit down and look at your financial needs and wants.

2. Take a good hard look at your lifestyle.

3. Look for ways to share your abundance with someone else.

4. Escape from dreamland. Dreamland is the thought that "when I get more money, then I'll start sharing."

4. **We are only stewards. The money really all belongs to God.** We brought nothing into this world, we will take nothing out. For a few short years in the meantime, God gives us the ability to be stewards of varying amounts of His resources.

5. The rich get richer. People repeat this phrase from generation to generation, only a few really understand why. The secret: Compound interest. Here's what I told David in my book to him. "If you can accumulate $10,000 in a savings account in the next four years and then let it grow at a 10 percent interest rate without any further additions for the next forty years, it will be worth $450,000. But it grows to $2.7 million at a 15 percent growth rate; and $14.7 million at 20 percent. Hopefully, at some point along the way, you would find ministries in which to profitably invest the interest to stop the stuff from piling up.

"Look at the same situation another way. Assume that you put $2,000 away into an untouchable account each year. At the end of forty years you would have $885,000 at a 10 percent return; $3.6 million at 15 percent; $14.7 million at 20 percent."

Two lessons here: First, the importance of sacrificing early in your career to start accumulating a capital base. The time value of money is incredibly important.

Second, the rate of return is important. Investing a portion of your savings in professionally-managed funds could add 5 percent to 10 percent to your yield. But, be careful. To get the higher returns, you almost always assume more risk.

6. Never buy today what you can put off until tomorrow. Every purchase that you delay for either a few weeks or a few months adds several dollars to your financial stability. Frequently, by delaying a purchase you completely change your mind about the investment. Since your spending has the opposite impact of compounding interest, you can quickly see the very high cost of making cumbersome spending commitments early in life.

7. Have a money plan. One of the best ways to delay

spending is to operate with a budget, buying only what you need. I'll underline that word "need". Use a budget, perhaps after Ron Blue's model which I've included at the start of this chapter. Notice in this budgeting model, giving and saving are withheld first along with taxes. Then the standard of living is determined from what's left.

Build in a schedule of giving generously and giving regularly. By doing so, you open up the storehouse of God's richest treasures when you give from a motive of love and faith. Some will be received while you're on Earth, but I'm convinced that many "dividends" will not be shown to you until you reach the judgment seat of Christ.

8. **Keep money in perspective.** Although we must be good stewards, the Bible warns against too much concern for money: "Do you want to be truly rich? You already are if you are happy and good. After all, we didn't bring any money with us when we came into the world, and we can't carry away a single penny when we die. So we should be well satisfied without money if we have enough food and clothing." (1 Timothy 6:6-8)

Most people determine their standard of living, then try to stretch their income to cover the bills. Giving gets squeezed down to a residual, rather than a top priority. That's why most people are deeply in debt and have lost their financial freedom and are not receiving spiritual blessings promised the generous giver.

"First, help me never to tell a lie. Second, give me neither poverty nor riches! Give me just enough to satisfy my needs! For if I grow rich, I may become content without God. And if I am too poor, I may steal, and thus insult God's holy name." (Proverbs 30:8-9)

11 Giving

How Much Blessing Can You Stand?

*Tell them to use their money to do good. They should
be rich in good works and should give happily to those
in need, always being ready to share with others
whatever God has given them. By doing this they will be
storing up real treasure for themselves in heaven—it is
the only safe investment for eternity! And they will be
living a fruitful Christian life down here as well.*

(1 Timothy 6:18-19)

*Happy is the generous man, the one who feeds the
poor.*

(Proverbs 22:9)

One evening when I was still a youngster, we were
sitting around the supper table. The family included your
Grandma and Grandpa Oster, your Great-Grandma Carrie
Smith, your Uncle Larry and me. Your grandmother, the
outstanding school teacher, who for 25 years taught hundreds of young men and women in New Hartford how to
read, was telling us about her day in school.

She told about this sweet little first-grade girl who had
the sniffles all winter because she "has holes in her shoes,
she has only a summer coat, and doesn't even have a
sweater to wear to school." She asked of my dad, "Harland,
what would you think about buying this little girl a pair of
shoes and a new coat?" Without debating for even a
moment, Dad responded, "I think we should do it."

79

That brief 5-minute exchange had a greater impact on my value system than a dozen lectures on sharing. The reason: I knew why my mother was working. Dad was struggling to make payments on the farm. The original 160-acre farm that your Great-Great-Grandfather Knud Oster had acquired from the homesteaders had been split up through financial difficulties when Grandpa Jim Oster was farming it. Dad had a chance to buy the 80 acres from Grandpa Jim and shortly thereafter was given an opportunity to buy the second 80 acres from a city investor. This brought the original Oster farm together again.

Although the objective of putting the home farm together was incredibly important to Dad and Mom, their love and compassion for others was even more important. They saw an opportunity to help someone in need, and they did.

That story doesn't end with giving. Several days later, Mother explained to us how happy this little girl was with her new shoes and her new coat. Both student and teacher had to keep their little secret from the other children to prevent jealousy in the class. It was a pleasure for all of us to hear the happy result of sharing.

I have no idea how many times Mother repeated her quiet act of generosity toward her students over the years. I know she left a legacy of love by investing above and beyond the minimum effort in teaching her children.

When I went to New Hartford High School, your grandmother was teaching first grade, and I was known as "Mrs. Oster's son, Merrill." Although I have written books, built companies, travelled the world, and done many "successful" things, whenever I return to New Hartford, one of the first questions people ask is, "How is your mom?" In New Hartford, I will always be "Mrs. Oster's son." She gave freely, not so much in money and clothes, but of herself to advance the cause of her students. Before they moved on to second grade those youngsters could read and read well, or Mom wasn't satisfied.

One neighbor boy who had difficulty in the first grade of another school visited our home frequently. Mom tutored him, built his confidence and sent him into second grade with new abilities.

Although the most important thing we have to give is ourselves, most people think of giving in financial terms. When I teach seminars on Biblical principles in business, I'm frequently confronted with, "Do I have to give at least ten percent? Ten percent of my gross? Or ten percent of my net?"

I was perplexed by those same questions as an early Christian. After listening to the late E. H. Matthias deliver a sermon on giving, I asked this businessman whether I should give ten percent of my gross or ten percent of my net. To this day, I've passed along his response: "Whatever you give, give from the heart. God will bless you for it. How much blessing can you stand?"

His statement broke me out of my legalistic thinking and got me on track toward giving as an exercise of love and commitment and vision, not one of wanting to meet God's minimum requirement.

Much has been said and written about what Jesus promised in Luke 6:38, "For if you give, you will get!" Many miss the real blessing in this promise by focusing on "getting" as their real objective. Giving with the motive of getting reduces this principle to a selfish, mechanical technique aimed at manipulating God.

The correct motive for giving is to please God. Our desire should be to carry out the loving work He has assigned us as His ambassadors. View this Biblical principle as a continuous cycle. Give, and when you receive, give more. When you receive more, give even more.

God has an abundant storehouse. But He frequently doesn't give us lots more until we give from what we already have. Guard against hoarding. Hoarding is the approach Satan uses. He told Eve, "Surely you can have that apple." The three basic attacks of Satan are aimed at getting for yourself: Lust of the eyes, lust of the flesh and pride of life.

So if you give money to a poor family and selfishly pray that God will give you a new Lincoln, you aren't in tune with God's plan. You are missing the whole point, and will likely miss the blessing which comes from giving with a servant's heart.

In his book, *Giving Yourself Away*, Larry O'Nan says, "You should always give with the goal of seeking to advance the work of God's kingdom here on earth." He offers seven steps in applying a Biblical approach to giving. He is referring to giving time, talent, possessions, and other gifts, as well as money. His suggested process:

1. Give yourself and your possessions to God by relinquishing all your rights.

2. Recognize that God is your total and final supply of all you need.

3. Count on Him by faith to empower you with the Holy Spirit. We can't live the life of a steward in our own strength.

4. Begin to give according to His directions.

5. Thank and praise God for the privilege you have of distributing His wealth and resources.

6. Expect results.

7. Give again and again and again.

Paul instructs believers, "Let each one do just as He proposed in His heart; not grudgingly or under compulsion; for God loves a cheerful giver." (2 Corinthians 9:7)

The Bible clearly teaches that God owns it all; we give from His abundant supply. We are to give cheerfully. When I have need, I am to ask Him. How I handle what He gives me is important because I reap what I sow.

The Old Testament is filled with examples of God's promised blessings being received in short order. However, in the New Testament we see both immediate and eternal rewards. It is for this reason we should not expect immediate tangible results and become discouraged if some hoped-for blessing doesn't show up. Perhaps part, or most, of the reward is being credited to our eternal account. In fact, Jesus encourages giving with eternal ends in mind: "Don't store up treasures here on earth where they can erode away or may be stolen. Store them in heaven where they will never lose their value, and are safe from thieves. If your profits are in heaven, your heart will be there, too." (Matthew 6:19-21)

12 Problems

There's an Opportunity Hidden Here

God is our refuge and strength, a tested help in times of trouble.

(Psalm 46:1)

Dear brothers, is your life full of difficulties and temptations? Then be happy, for when the way is rough, your patience has a chance to grow.

(James 1:2-3)

I think I know why you aren't enthusiastic about camping trips. When you were 10 years old, your mom and I packed you and Dave in the camper immediately after school. We headed for Howard County on an evening mushroom hunt.

After the hunt, we stopped beside a cow pasture along the Upper Iowa River. I crossed an electric fence to get some sticks for our bonfire. The electric fence had a mild tickle, just enough to discourage the cows from leaning on the fence.

You decided to follow me. Just as you touched the fence, Mom slammed the door of the motor home. The simultaneous electric jolt and noise of the door slamming

sent you leaping and screaming! It took a few minutes on
your mother's lap before you regained your composure.

The way you solved that potential problem was to
forever avoid electric fences and to take a dim view of
living in a cow pasture, even for an evening.

When you've faced really big problems, you've dealt
with them head-on. I like that. You have the courage to
enlist the prayer support of people around you. You recognize the power of tapping spiritual resources. Then you
also muster every possible personal resource available in
you. You do a great job of balancing obedience and dependence on God against using the personal strengths
God has already given you. In the solution to every problem, there is usually God's portion and man's portion.

God doesn't want us to sit slothfully and pray for
miraculous solutions to problems when he has already
given us the minds and muscles to handle the challenge.
He gave many direct commands to action: "Follow me."
"Do it." On the other hand, He doesn't want us to arrogantly roll up our sleeves with an "I'll do it my way"
attitude. Our Lord's attitude was one of "not my will, but
Thine." Our confidence must come from a dependence
on God, not on our own limited strength.

You had a big problem when, as a Taylor University
freshman, you wanted to get closer to home and be on the
same campus with your brother at Wheaton College. The
Wheaton admissions office didn't look too kindly on your
first semester grades. That was the semester when you
learned there was quite a difference between preparing for
high school and college tests. I recall talking through the
steps with you as you sized up the problem and planned
your strategy. We all prayed. You received a one-semester
conditional transfer. Then part of your strategy was to
politely "bug" the Wheaton registrar's office so much that

you became their problem. You showed your face often enough in the admissions office to prove you had desire. Finally, armed with another semester of good grades and a promise that you were going to be a good student, you achieved your objective. You made good on your promise to the admissions department by earning good grades all through college.

Some problems, or trials, weigh heavily on the mind because they are not as clearly solved as your college admissions problem. I would like to suggest a logical way to address a problem, keep it in perspective and focus your God-given resources. This problem-solving format also helps make your prayers more specific:

Problem solving exercise

1. Is it a problem — or a condition?

A general layoff that involves 1,000 people, of whom you are one, is a *condition* in the work force over which you probably have little control. However, a performance review by your superior that says you will lose your job if you don't improve your performance is a solvable *problem*. Start by asking if this situation is really a problem, or a general condition to which you may have to adapt. Often, people blame themselves for conditions beyond their control. The resulting guilt and worry drains their ability to cope.

2. Clearly state the problem in writing.

The exercise of putting a problem down in writing often reduces it to specific words which help remove or isolate emotional confusion. A problem *clearly stated* is usually a problem half solved.

3. State the causes.

By identifying the causes, you begin to immediately

think about what some of the solutions might be.

4. State what will be gained or lost by solving the problem.

Sometimes the answer to this question results in a gain or loss so ridiculously small that you admit the problem is not really a problem at all.

5. List each alternative and the cost of each.

Most problem situations can be solved in a variety of approaches. By listing the alternatives you think are available and the approximate cost in energy, emotions, friendships and money, you prepare to seriously weigh the choices.

6. Select the best alternative.

Often it is not clear which route is best. But by selecting one and moving ahead confidently, the size of the problem is usually reduced immediately.

7. Spell out what action is required to implement the chosen alternative.

Sometimes a simple problem requires only one action. However, a more complex problem may have five to seven steps that need to be worked through before a final solution is found. Obviously, the best action on any problem is to pray and enlist the prayer support of others.

Keep a record of solved problems. Your successes in problem-solving will help you deal with future problems in this logical step-by-step fashion instinctively, without even using a piece of paper. You internalize the process and become a good problem solver. Your list of solved problems builds your confidence in God and the abilities He gave you. Unsolved problems can remain on your prayer list. They may require the advice of someone who has been through similar situations.

I do not suggest, however, that all problems can be solved. Some just won't go away. These unresolved problems become the trials that really test our faith and build our patience. We learn to adapt, to live with them, to minimize them and to continually pray that God will help us work through them.

In every problem you face, always hold the expectation that somewhere beneath the surface lies an opportunity. Once you have mustered the energy to solve the problem, just keep right on working to see if there isn't an advantage to be gained by turning a negative situation into a positive one.

Problems turned into great blessings for the apostles who wrote the prison epistles. *Pilgrim's Progress* is the result of John Bunyan's problem of imprisonment.Charles Colson says he wouldn't trade his days in prison, when he intensely studied the Bible, for all the time he spent in the White House. Businessmen have repeatedly told me their financial struggles were the "best thing that ever happened" to them because they learned to trust the Lord. One businessman's wife wrote as I was completing this chapter. Her family had lost everything, but she said, "My husband and I are Christians, a fact that we do not take lightly after the last three years. We believe that nothing happens to us that has not been permitted by the hand of God. We see that God has brought growth and maturity to us through this seeming calamity."

While I was attending college at Iowa State University, I saw God turn a problem into a tremendous opportunity in my life. I had an early morning radio announcing job. On the way home from the radio station, I met a classmate who told me my fraternity house was on fire. That sounded like a joke. I didn't really believe him until a second person, with fear in her eyes, said, "Merrill, there's smoke coming out of your house!" I broke into a run and got to the house to find firemen on two floors. Smoke poured out of the roof. I tried to get to my room, but the firemen said it was too late.

Later we learned the fire had started in the basement, two floors below my room by spontaneous combustion of rags used to clean paint brushes. Fortunately, my roommate was away at a student teaching assignment and had most of his clothes with him. However, I lost all my clothes. I drove home with a few smokey remains to have them washed. Your Grandma and Grandpa Oster bought enough new clothes for me so I could return to school.

Most of the fellows in my fraternity were able to find temporary housing in one location. There wasn't room for everyone, so I spent three or four days searching for an extra bed in Ames.

Finally, I met a friend on campus who said there was one bed left in the house where he stayed. Craig Simcox, a Christian friend from home, told me there were two other Christian men in the house. I moved in. I got involved in their Bible studies. I spent time in prayer with those men in the new house. I went to church with them on Sundays. I stayed in that house for the next 18 months because those Christian mentors had such a positive influence on my life.

What had appeared on the surface to be a negative experience — losing my living quarters and all my clothes — turned out to be a vitally important event in my life. At the time of the fire, I had reduced my church attendance to "whenever it was convenient." My prayer life was spotty at best. Although I witnessed occasionally when someone challenged my beliefs, I certainly was not actively reaching out to serve the Lord.

The encouragement of other Christian men was tremendously helpful. They prayed each night before they went to bed. They made a deep impression on me, a dramatic impact on the direction of my life at a critical time. I had been caught up by secular busyness, and no doubt could have been swept away from an interest in spiritual things if the Lord had not gotten my attention after the fire.

From time to time, the Lord will send little bonfires into your life. And from time to time you will create some of your own. But, even through those self-inflicted trials, God uses these experiences to deepen his relationship with you. He's ready to use a negative event as a positive influence in your life. I have seen so many negative situations turned into positive ones in my life that when a new problem shows up, I sometimes get nervous with anticipation, wondering what good thing God is going to bring this time.

Your trials in life will be exercises that strengthen you for tasks ahead. In a very real sense, each trial is like a distance run. Each run builds your strength to win an even longer one. That's how the marathoners train.

The best thing about the marathon of the Christian life is that we know that we finish — and we win! The victory is eternal life.

13   Prayer

Reach for Your Power Cord

Ye have not because ye ask not.

(James 4:2)

And so it is with prayer — keep on asking and you will keep on getting; keep on looking and you will keep on finding; knock and the door will be opened. Everyone who asks, receives; all who seek, find; and the door is opened to everyone who knocks.

(Luke 11: 9-10)

You and your brother David had a few strong verbal disagreements while you were growing up. Fortunately, you grew out of that period and became best of friends. I remember one day when the two of you clashed with such enthusiasm that you wouldn't speak to each other — or even look at each other! At breakfast you lined up cereal boxes on the table to block David out of your sight.

That night, as all four of us gathered at the foot of your bed for prayer, Mom asked for prayer requests. You and David each volunteered a desire to get along better with the other. We took that request, along with others, to the Lord in prayer. Then, as usual we sat on the floor and chatted a few minutes. The two of you began talking. You apologized to each other. Finally, you ended the day by telling each other, "I love you."

A few moments in the presence of Almighty God had a powerful and practical impact on our lives that day and on many, many subsequent occasions. My encouragement is to build on past successes. Praise God for what He has done for you. When you speak with God in an attitude of praise, the problems of the day and even sharp differences between individuals can melt into obscurity.

I suggest you continue to use prayer as a way to maintain open lines of communication with other people as well as with God. When you pray, you plug into a spiritual power source. This power helps you see situations from God's perspective. You tap the most awesome power in the universe — the power of the Holy Spirit. It's available to anyone who is willing to acknowledge Jesus Christ as Lord. The Lord promises to hear and answer prayer. Prayer can release tension between you and other people, resolving conflicts with love and forgiveness.

When you bring God, the ever-present source of peace and comfort, into the gap between two people, they can reevaluate things in the light of the greatness of God's love and grace. He forgave us everything! By comparison, our interpersonal problems are dwarfed by God's love. When we pray, we acknowledge God's right to live through us. Then, with His strength, we ask for and offer forgiveness.

I must confess to you that my prayer time is a lot more intent when I'm trapped in some crisis that seems impossible. The peace you enjoy in life will, to a large extent, depend upon how well you learn to use prayer power in every situation, large or small.

The Lord expects us to come to Him boldly. One of the boldest prayers in Scripture was offered by one of its least-known people, Jabez. He appears in Scripture very briefly in 1 Chronicles 4:9-10. He prayed, "Oh, that you would wonderfully bless me and help me in my work; please be with me in all that I do, and keep me from all evil and disaster!" And God granted him his request:

1. God's blessing was poured out to him.

2. God enlarged his borders — no doubt his sphere of influence — as well.

3. God protected him in an evil world.

4. God kept His hand on Jabez, freeing him from the power of sin.

A believing prayer, like that of Jabez, is an indication of our faith. When you ask God's help, you align yourself with the strongest force in the universe.

The starting point in effective prayer is knowing that Christ is in your life. Jesus said, "You must be born again." The next step is to express your willingness to allow Him to take charge. In the first step, you acknowledge Jesus as Savior. Then by your words, attitude and actions you acknowledge Him as Lord of your total life.

Prayer is the way God provided for Christians to tie into His power. This all-important principle is laid out in Luke 11:13, "And if even sinful persons like yourselves give children what they need, don't you realize that your heavenly Father will do at least as much, and give the Holy Spirit to those who ask for Him?"

In John 20:22, the Lord speaks not about the indwelling of the Holy Spirit which takes place when a person receives Christ. Instead, the Lord speaks of that daily renewing of power, frequently called the "filling of the Holy Spirit," which comes only as we ask.

God gives the power of his Holy Spirit to those who

ask! Since we can't live the Christian life by our own power, your daily request to be empowered by the Holy Spirit is like recharging your batteries.

Sometimes we slip into discouragement, stress and depression even while we busily empty ourselves in Christian service. Spiritual weakness may result from sin, but it can also result from a broken connection with God in Bible reading and prayer. Church attendance helps, but it can't substitute for personal contact. A prayer which asks God for His power and praises Him for His person is a needed recharger.

Prayer is the trigger point of true joy. Jesus replied in John 16:24, "Ask, using My name, and you will receive, and your cup of joy will overflow." Christians ought to be happy. That's God plan. But we can abort this plan and live defeated lives with unmet needs by trying to do things in our own strength. Jesus hands you His calling card in this verse and says, in effect, "Feel free to use My name when calling on God." It's a powerful knock on God's door when your opening words of prayer say, "I'm calling in the name of the Lord Jesus Christ, your Son."

Prayer is also the road out of trouble. We can make a trade — our worries for real peace! Philippians 4:6-7 says, "Don't worry about anything, instead, pray about everything, tell God your needs and don't forget to thank Him for His answers. If you do this you will experience God's peace, which is far more wonderful than the human mind can understand."

God's prescription for anxiety, for fear about the future, for worry is prayer. 1 Peter 5:7 restates the same command: "Cast all your cares upon Him, for He cares for you."

Prayer builds a fence of protection that shields you

from temptation. "Watch and pray, lest you enter into temptation. The spirit truly is ready, but the flesh is weak." (Mark 14:38) When we fix our eyes on the Lord in prayer, we aren't about to be diverted by Satan's constant deceit. Next to running away from temptation, regular prayer is the best remedy for enticements from the powers of darkness.

Prayer deepens your relationship with God. As you talk to God, pause to quietly listen. Do you hear the rattling skeleton of an unconfessed sin? If so, confess it. Ask God's forgiveness. Do you feel the estrangement caused by a lack of fellowship with another believer? Drop what you are doing and "go make it right with your brother."

Then ask Him. Praise Him. Beseech Him on behalf of others. Worship Him. Make prayer your first and last act of every day, and your frequent activity during the day.

The God who poured out blessings and performed miracles from Genesis to Revelation is the same God to whom you pray today. If we don't get the results of the men of old, it is a reflection on our lack of faith, not on God. He hasn't changed. A popular poster suggests, "Do you feel far from God? Guess who moved!"

The Psalmist acknowledged, "O thou that hearest prayer, unto thee shall all flesh come." The same God who heard David's prayer is waiting for your prayers to unlock His storehouse of blessings.

The Lord urged, "If ye shall ask anything in My name, I will do it." How often our prayer is for self-centered things. Charles A. Blanchard, writer of *Getting Things From God,* says: "Praying in the name of Jesus is praying in order that the name of Jesus may be glorified ... but if I do not pray that He may be glorified — only that I may be eased and comforted — what object would He have in answering my prayer?"

So, one of my great hopes for you is that you become a woman who grows in prayer. You and I will never know to what degree our contribution in life is attributed to the praying women around us. But I can guarantee that as you become a stronger woman of prayer, you will join a chain of women who have already prayed fervently for you and me — your mother, your grandmothers, and your great-grandmothers.

Long before she passed away, your great-grandmother, Bessie Oster, said, "I just praise the Lord that all my kiddies are saved." Although she had lost her husband and a son, your great-grandma expressed a great attitude of praise and thanksgiving. Great-Grandma Oster didn't have a lot of this world's "things" to be thankful for. She lived a life of hard work on the farm, and a very simple life with meager belongings in retirement. Finally, she had only one small roomful of pictures and personal things in a nursing home.

One of my cherished memories of Great-Grandma Bessie comes from her late years. I walked into her room at the nursing home. There she sat in a state of prayer: Wrinkled hands clasped against her brow weathered by time and outdoor work. What a beautiful memory of your Great-Grandmother Bessie Oster!

And, your Great-Grandmother Carrie Smith prayed for your salvation, even before you were born. Although her memory is slipping, her interest in you and David is always a part of our conversation. I know the legacy of the praying women in your family tree will be your legacy, too!

14 Crisis

If I'm So Successful, Why Do I Hurt?

Don't worry about anything; instead, pray about everything; tell God your needs and don't forget to thank him for his answers. If you do this you will experience God's peace, which is far more wonderful than the human mind can understand. His peace will keep your thoughts and your hearts quiet and at rest as you trust in Christ Jesus.

(Philippians 4:6-7)

My help is from Jehovah who made the mountains! And the heavens too! He will never let me stumble, slip or fall.

(Psalm 121:2-3)

The Lord is a strong fortress. The godly run to him and are safe.

(Proverbs 18:10)

Your life temporarily stood still yesterday afternoon. You learned that your friend stepped in front of a train, apparently taking his own life. A young life, whose voice extended a daily greeting to you, was instantly snuffed out.

Although your mom and I knew the young man only as an acquaintance, we shed our tears with you at this time of grief and distress. My heart is heavy as I write. I sense the

99

emptiness that must grip you at this moment. As I mentioned on the phone, although our words of comfort to each other are appreciated, the ultimate source of comfort is Jesus Christ, our Comforter. At all times, but especially during crisis, we must seek the face of God the Father through His Son Jesus Christ.

One time when we were out at Aunt Theo and Uncle Ray's house, you walked over to a neighbor's yard and stuck your finger through the wires of a cage, trying to touch the pet rabbit. You weren't quite two years old yet, so you were startled when the rabbit jumped over to the edge of the cage and nibbled at your finger with his tender lips. The combined quick move of the rabbit and the nibbling at your fingertips sent you into frightened shock. You ran as fast as you could over to the lawn chair where I was sitting. You curled up in my arms and sobbed and sobbed. After a few minutes of hearing my reassuring words, you were smiling again even though your face was wet with tears.

Some of the crises we face in life, like the tragedy today, have no adequate explanation. Just as my arms comforted you when you were a baby, God wants you to depend on Him today. In prayer you can "let your hair down" before God. Tell Him your feelings. Although your mom and I are as close as the nearest telephone, God's promise is to be with you always to comfort, strengthen and guide.

The apostle Paul assured us, "He is . . . the source of every mercy, and . . . is the One Who wonderfully comforts and strengthens us in our hardships and trials." (2 Corinthians 1:3,4) "And why does he do this? So that when others are troubled, needing our sympathy and encouragement, we can pass on to them this same help and comfort God has given us. You can be sure that the more we undergo sufferings for Christ, the more he will shower us with His comfort and encouragement." (2 Corinthians 1:4,5) He adds in verse 7, "He will give you the strength to endure." Chuck Swindoll in his book, *For Those Who Hurt*, says about these verses, "This is no shallow sympathy card with rhyming words and gold-glitter greeting. It is eternally more than a 'slap on the back' or a quick 'Cheer up,' bit of advice. Our mighty God is called alongside as we suffer! Here is genuine comfort, personal assistance, deep involvement and an infinite understanding."

I sense this Word of God is providing comfort to your friend's parents and family, and to his friends at this moment.

Interspersed among life's pleasant moments are a series of trials, crises, shocks, disappointments and other seemingly negative events.

I know one thing for sure: When I go through one of these events, the first thing I do after talking to the Lord about it is to share it with your mother. Then I often find a friend or acquaintance who has been through a similar problem. That friend's words come from an understanding point of view. His perspective is shaped by "having been there."

Even this terrible experience you are going through is in some way preparing you to show comfort and love to someone else in the future. Having been there yourself, you can understand.

You experienced yesterday that there is a time during terrible crisis when words are unnecessary. By getting together with other friends and weeping yesterday afternoon and evening, you shared each other's grief at such a depth that only your presence was needed. In the future, when someone else is going through deep grief, you will know that your presence will bring comfort to another.

Having been there, you'll know when it's time for a few well-chosen words.

"Tears have a language all their own," Swindoll continues. "When words fail, tears flow. In some mysterious way, our complex inner-communication system knows when to admit its verbal limitations . . . and the tears come. Eyes that flashed and sparkled only moments before are floated from a secret reservoir. We try in vain to restrain the flow, but even strong men falter."

In your tears yesterday, you spoke volumes that only God could interpret. In Psalm 56:8 we are assured that He takes our tears, bottles them up, and records them. Your tears summoned the attention of the King of Kings and Lord of Lords.

A. W. Tozer has said, "It is doubtful whether God can bless a man greatly until He has hurt him deeply."

The Lord is a strong fortress. The godly run to him and are safe.

(Proverbs 18:10)

15 Others

Happiness Is a By-Product of Service

*Don't be selfish; don't live to make a good impression
on others. Be humble, thinking of others as better than
yourself. Don't just think about your own affairs, but be
interested in others, too, and in what they are doing.*
(Philippians 2:3-4)

As the Mercedes limousine pull·d up to London's
Westminster Abbey, a group of curious bystanders was
surprised to see a nine-year-old girl step out of the back
seat, escorted by the driver on this tour of historic spots.
You were getting the royal treatment!

Because the U.S. dollar was strong at the time, the
ride didn't cost much more than a taxi fare in Chicago. Yet
the special treatment you received that morning made a
life-long impression on you. At each historic site, the driver
opened the door for you and took you to the point of
interest. He asked you how long you wanted to stay, what
you liked to do, and made his time and car totally available
to you for the morning.

When you rejoined me at the convention I was attending, your eyes danced. You had a series of stories about your personally-escorted tour of London.

That afternoon we took a long walking tour of the city and had a great time together. But the memory that always flashes back to you of our father-daughter London trip is the royal treatment in the chauffeured limo. (And, the uneven pigtails I had made in your hair, as I tried to be both mother and father for a week.)

We all have within us a mechanism which desires the "royal treatment." Often, it doesn't take a major effort to give another person that kind of treatment. Just showing interest is enough. Sometimes, just remembering another person's name is all it takes to make a lasting impression.

Twenty years ago, I led a delegation of businessmen to India, Pakistan and Thailand to study the world food situation. I met a Colorado man on this trip. Ten years passed before I heard from Bill again. He called me at home one evening. The voice said, "Hello, Merrill. Do you have any idea who this is?" The qualities of Bill's voice hit my memory button in a flash and I said, "Why yes, how are you, Bill?" He was amazed and pleased that I remembered his name.

Last week at a seminar in Nebraska, I saw Bill again. Ten years had passed since that telephone call. Bill sought me out at the end of the seminar and said "Merrill, I was absolutely amazed that you remembered my voice when I called you ten years ago." Bill is typical of most of us. We like to be remembered.

Taking an interest in other people and remembering them in various ways is one of the natural results of Christianity. Many forces in our society press us in the opposite direction. Best-selling books and professional improvement seminars today promote serving self rather than serving others. I want to encourage you to continue an interest in others and give their needs high priority in your life.

Dale Carnegie's best seller *How to Win Friends and Influence People* has had a timeless impact on generations. He explains principles first laid out in the Sermon on the Mount. In that sermon in Matthew 5:5, the Lord said, "The meek and lowly are fortunate! For the whole wide world belongs to them." In verse 7 the Lord said, "Happy are the kind and merciful, for they shall be shown mercy."

It is significant that these beatitudes, or the attitudes for proper service, are written in the context of a world mission. In verses 14 through 16 the Lord's words are, "You are the world's light — a city on a hill, glowing in the night for all to see. Don't hide your light! Let it shine for all; let your good deeds glow for all to see, so that they will praise your Heavenly Father."

The Carnegie book is written to show how life is more successful when you take an interest in others. The beatitudes are written to show how we find eternal significance in God's eternal plan to reach mankind when we put the interest of others first.

In today's busy world with the enormous thrust towards self-centeredness, people who consistently show loving care for other people are noticed quickly because they are different from most others around them. They are beacon lights of hope who attract other people to a relationship with Jesus Christ.

There are some very practical ways this concept makes a difference in business. Business basically has four elements: 1) customers; 2) a needed product or service; 3) employees; and 4) suppliers. The most successful companies today are customer-driven. The ex-

ecutives spend time listening to customers. Their re-
searchers respond to customer demands. The customer
is always considered more important than the products
sold. Without customers, there is no business.

Giving good customer service can be a *learned* business technique. But the most sincere and meaningful
customer service is that which comes as a natural out-
growth of an inner desire to follow Christ's example and
serve others. Our goal is to pattern our work after the
example our Lord gave us.

Successful companies also listen carefully to their
employees. One of the first things I do when interviewing
potential business associates is to find out about them as
people. In that way, I can begin to learn what makes up
their value system, what drives them, what their most
important goals are. Only when I am convinced that our
job description is one that will help the prospective business associate achieve his or her goals do I move to an in-
depth interview and a discussion of specific skills. Usually,
this results in adapting a job description to the individual's
talents and interests.

A product or service sold to the customer should be
developed with the same attitude. A continual challenge to
my associates is to see how much value we can provide at
the very lowest possible price. That's a common sense
business idea that is Biblically based. Our products and
services are designed with customers' advice, are tested
by customers, and upgraded based on improvements
suggested by customers.

Suppliers are the fourth major component of a business. Showing an interest in their needs makes them an
integral part of a team that can best serve the customers'
needs. Suppliers of everything from money to software,
hardware, paper and printing deserve the same "royal

treatment" we give our business associates and our customers.

If we serve others strictly to manipulate them, our motivation shows through and we are seen as a superficial, back-slapping, glad-handing people. But if you carry your true motivation of service to others to the workplace, even when you can expect nothing in return, the response is, "She is a genuine person!" This is already your reputation. My words only reaffirm what is already being established in your life.

I like what Dale Carnegie says about serving others:

CARNEGIE'S SIX WAYS TO MAKE PEOPLE LIKE YOU

Rule 1: Become genuinely interested in other people.

Rule 2: Smile.

Rule 3: Remember that a man's name is to him the sweetest and most important sound in any language.

Rule 4: Be a good listener and encourage them to talk about themselves.

Rule 5: Talk in terms of the other person's interest.

Rule 6: Make the other person feel important — and do it sincerely.

It was Henry Ford who said, "If there is any one secret to success, it lies in the ability to get the other person's point of view and see things from his angle as well as from your own."

Our Lord's life was centered on others, not on Himself. He came to seek and to save the lost (Luke 19:10), not to live for His own pleasure. "He laid down his life for us, and we are to lay down our lives for the brethren," says 1

John 3:16. As David Hocking says in *Pleasing God*, "Allowing self — that is, our sinful nature — to be pleased, pampered, coddled and stroked means we cannot please God. To be selfish means we are consumed with our own needs. In that state of mind, we easily doubt that God cares."

Alan Loy McGinnis reaffirms this point in his book, *Bringing Out the Best in People*: "You are a manipulator when you try to persuade people to do something that is not in their best interest but is in yours. You are a motivator when you find goals that will be good for both sides, then weld together a high-achieving, high-moral partnership to achieve them."

16 Marriage

What You See Is What You Get, So Look!

So again I say, a man must love his wife as a part of himself; and the wife must see to it that she deeply respects her husband — obeying, praising and honoring him.

(Ephesians 5:33)

As a 4- or 5-year old, you made the announcement one night, "Daddy, when I grow up I want to marry you!" I responded, "You know when you are married, there are responsibilities like Mommy has — washing dishes, cleaning the house..." You didn't bat an eye in coming back, "Then how 'bout we just be good friends?"

Thoughts of marriage enter our lives at a very early age, because marriage is God's answer to our loneliness. In all likelihood, you will marry. I have a few ideas you should consider:

Ideally, the man you choose to be your husband ought to feel secure as a person. He should understand his true significance from God's point of view. He will

111

exhibit confidence and security in various ways through his personality and conversation. You can spot an insecure man by the way he talks about himself and other people. If he is constantly putting someone else down to make himself look good, it's a warning that he doesn't feel good about himself.

If you see an enormous number of signals that the young man in question is insecure and immature, don't hope for a miracle. Chances are, what you see is what you will get. Although God can change lives in miraculous ways, He only does so in those who make themselves totally available to Him. Be prepared to live with every wart you notice while you are dating.

There's a big difference between cocky self-assuredness and a quiet, humble self-confidence that has deep roots. The cocky, arrogant, fast-talking, brash young man is usually holding up an enormous mask, covering insecurities and problems in his life that create unrealistic expectations or problems in other relationships, including marriage.

In his book, *The Marriage Builder*, Lawrence J. Crabb, Jr. says the goal of marriage should be to develop a deep experience of personal intimacy through relationship with a person of the opposite sex. Crabb says, "I understand the Scriptures to teach that relationship offers two elements which are absolutely essential if we are to live as God intended: (1) the security of being truly loved and accepted, and (2) the significance of making a substantial, lasting, positive impact on another person." Crabb calls security and significance the Master's provisions. "We are not intended to function according to the Master's plan without first equipping ourselves with the Master's provision," he says. The starting point for love and security is a proper understanding of where we stand as Christians.

God's Word assures us that in Christ we are both secure in His love and are significant beings in His eternal plan for mankind.

We can build a feeling of real security when we understand who we are in Christ. This understanding is the bedrock upon which a relationship must be built. Says Crabb, "A wife who feels desperately insecure is quite capable of giving herself to her husband if she believes she is secure in Christ. A husband who feels threatened by his wife's rejection is responsible for lovingly accepting her because he can believe he is a worthwhile Christian regardless of his wife's response."

This whole concept of security and significance is so important in understanding people, I really want you to hear it from an expert. Crabb is the best I've read.

Now, some thoughts straight from Dad: Watch out for the macho man. He's usually wearing a big mask covering up for his insecurities or feelings of insignificance. The macho man is usually so devoted to manhood, that he cannot appreciate the tender feelings and subtle sensitivities of a woman.

Love at first sight probably isn't. Since the true definition of love is being willing to serve another in a sacrificial way, it's very unlikely that some handsome prince is going to sweep into your life and prove worthy of your service in a matter of hours. The emotion at first sight is more likely to be physically motivated than spiritually.

Since you're going to spend the rest of your life with the man of your choice, you'd better make sure you share a broad number of interests. That doesn't mean your interests and his should have a 100 percent, or even an 80 percent, matchup — but there should be ample common ground for good conversation and participation. And, your areas of common interests should overlap some of the most important interests in your life. Check with each other on such areas as financial philosophy, lifestyle desires, giving goals, family size and other issues that are important to your future.

Although your mother and I have quite different athletic interests, we have common interests on the important goals of how we want the major part of our lives to serve the Lord. Early in our dating we compared and shared our views on church and doctrinal matters, relative interests in children, how to discipline them, and our relative roles.

The role question is an even bigger one today. Twenty-five years ago, there seemed to be no trouble with men accepting the role of decision-maker and leader in the family. Today's feminist movement has provided some horrible role models for both young men and women. The increase in divorce has also contributed to the problem. The result is confusion in today's young marrieds over who is to lead and how, and who is to follow and when.

As you know, I feel strongly that the male role is one of initiator, and the female role is one of responder. Just as Christ is head of the church, man is to be the head of the woman. Marriage is God's way of presenting the world with a picture of Jesus Christ and His church. Families led by dominant women with weak men following their lead tend to produce brassy girls. The boys from such a marriage tend to be wimpy guys who can't lead, are afraid to make decisions and appear to have no direction. They simply are unprepared to play their Biblical role in marriage because it wasn't acted out in their homes.

As a "helpmate," your strengths of personality and character should complement your husband's, not compete. A wise man will be able to use his strengths and yours to make him a better leader and decision maker.

Think about the young men on a scale of self-centeredness versus an orientation toward others. You are sensitive enough to pick up the signals of a self-centered man in the first 15 minutes of conversation. To whom does he point the flow of conversation? To what degree does he take a sincere interest in you, your feelings, your goals, and your strengths?

It's a good idea to understand the young man's relationship with his parents. If there are seeds of bitterness or rebellion against his parents, you're looking at a potential powder keg.

You will get some clues on whether or not a young man will be a good husband by getting a picture of where he's been, and where he appears to be going relative to what he says his goals are. A young man chasing rainbows and talking pipe dreams in his mid-20's will still be doing it in his mid-40's. If he says he is serious about serving the Lord, there should be some evidence now. There should be a pattern of serving God in various ways, perhaps well back into his high school years to provide verification of his words. Be wary of the fellow whose goals appear to be so far out of reach in relationship to what he's already accomplished, that he might not have an accurate understanding of who he really is.

You have a great sense of humor, an ability to laugh at yourself and laugh with others. It seems to make sense that the man you marry should be able to understand the humor in many of the things you do. You don't want to laugh alone.

You probably already have an excellent idea of the personality traits and characteristics of the man you hope to marry. I would suggest you commit that list to paper, and ask the Lord about the list and the man with your desired qualities. This list will help you sort through your emotions to come up with a decision formed both by the head and the heart. While you are waiting for that man to march into your life, God will no doubt work on those characteristics in your own life as he prepares your heart for this very important meeting. I have a feeling that when the right man comes into your life, after a period of dating you will have your own sense of where God is leading you. He will begin to give you peace on the questions that you raise in regard to this young man. At the same time, he will no doubt be verifying your direction through the counsel of other people around you, perhaps your friends, your parents and his parents.

It's pretty hard to play out a cookie-cutter approach to the selection of a mate. Each situation is a bit unique. Your mother and I knew each other from the time we were eight or ten years old (she reminds me that when I was ten she was seven). Our parents were good friends. Our upbringing gave us a similar understanding and appreciation of Biblical truths.

We dated for the first time in my senior year in college. I gave her a ride home on a cold January night, then reopened the conversation at my brother's high school graduation in May. We dated from May through August. Since I had a few weeks totally free, we spent lots of time together. We saw each other in various situations from attending church to visiting historic sites and caves to a day at the Iowa State Fair where I did some free-lance journalism work. We double-dated with some good friends, and spent lots of time with our parents on picnics and in conversations around the kitchen tables.

I took no chance of losing your mom after that wonderful summer. I asked her to marry me just before I left for

Madison, Wisconsin, to get my master's degree in journalism. We wrote, travelled one direction or the other on many weekends, and married the following June.

Although the time between our first serious date and our wedding was only a little more than a year, our long-time knowledge of each other made getting acquainted much easier. Obviously, I'd recommend a few more months of dating. (I know, this is "do as I say, not as I do" advice.)

Since I'm a businessman and not a full-time Christian counsellor, you'll have to accept these words as from Dad, not from a marriage expert. However, I can recommend some outstanding authors on this topic: Elizabeth Elliott, *Let Me Be A Woman*; Don Meredith, *Becoming One*; Josh McDowell, *The Secret of Loving*; and, Ed Wheat, *Love Life*.

At least once a year, your mom and I attend a Christian seminar that devotes a serious portion of its time to marriage. We're still learning.

If you pattern yourself after your mom, which you already have, and if you apply yourself to your marriage as hard as your mother has, you're going to be one fantastic wife. I am confident that when the consideration of this topic hits the top level on your priority list, you'll be able to discern between a phony and the real thing, between the proud and the humble, between the self-centered and the other-centered, between the tender-spirited, sensitive person and the harsh, insensitive person.

More important than this chapter of advice, you'll have that "still small voice" whispering to you, guiding you, encouraging you to make the right choice. With God as your guide, the only big mistake you can make is not listening to Him, or confusing His encouraging with your own emotions.

Somehow I see figuring into this whole decision-making process a picture of you and your mom sitting up late some night, talking in quiet tones so you don't interrupt my sleep. But if you need me, just give a gentle holler down the hall, and I'll join in, too.

17 Significance

Avoid the "Good" for the Best

It is God Himself who has made us what we are and given us new lives from Christ Jesus; and long ages ago He planned that we should spend these lives in helping others.

(Ephesians 2:10)

As I filled the water softener with salt last night, I paused in the basement by your old toy box. It's still filled with toys which, at various times, occupied the center of your attention. There is a row of ducks you pulled by a string to hear the quackity, quackity sound. Little kids who visit our place today really enjoy that old toy. Other reminders of your past include Barbie dolls, teacups and saucers that made up your full setting for four when you wanted to play house, a toy piano which struck your fancy at about age five, and a closet full of dolls.

Your interest moved from toys and dolls on to radios, stereos, bicycles, and finally cars. Each group of "toys" is a reminder of a growing mind and changing values. At each stage in life, you considered a new set of things to be really important.

The apostle Paul in Philippians 3:8 must have had some of the "toys" of his life in mind when he said, "Compared to knowing Christ, all of this other stuff is nothing but rubbish" (my own paraphrase). When I read that verse, it sends my mind to the rubbish heaps, or "junk piles" of my youth.

I used to find really good stuff in the family "junk pile" as an 8-year-old. Every farm family had a spot where anything that wouldn't burn was piled — from tin cans to old refrigerators and washers to broken pieces of farm equipment.

Rummaging through that junk pile, you could find a few old buggy wheels, maybe a large wooden plank, some old rope, and a broomstick. With a few other odds and ends and a few bolts from Dad's workbench, a young boy could put together a go-cart that would coast down hills or could be pushed down a ramp for some afternoon racing thrills.

But the old family junk pile lost its appeal after I spotted a huge junk pile a mile from home — the county dump. Laws today don't allow such open dumps. But then, the county dump was a place where even city folks would toss their throwaways. I was always amazed at how much good stuff city folks threw away.

On a typical afternoon walk across the section to the county dump, I would come back with two 5-gallon pails full of "good stuff." I mean really good stuff — ball bearings from farm machines that could be turned into "steelies" in a game of marbles. Lamps that actually worked. Shovels, rakes, and other tools that needed just a little fixing. A trip to the county dump always provided a pleasant "find."

When I turned 16, I bought a 1949 Chevy for $365.

My attention shifted. This time I found a new junkyard — Aikey's Salvage Yard. That was a place where I could go to find inexpensive additions to the car; a spinner to turn the steering wheel faster, mud flaps to look "cool" and equipment to lower the car's rear end. It was always fun to see how much good stuff you could find for five bucks at Aikey's. Even after I left home for college, I would occasionally come home and find a part at Aikey's to keep that Chevy running.

Then, a couple of years later, just before you were born, we bought a new car. From that time on, I never was interested in any of the former junk piles of my life.

For many people, life is only a process of seeking bigger and better "junk piles." You've probably seen the bumper sticker, "He who retires with the most toys, wins." Christians are freed from that disappointing dead end. We gear ourselves and all the important things in life to eternal values. It's easy to get distracted by a new influence in life and temporarily put things of the Lord in second place. The thrill of dating the man you think will be "Mr. Right," then, making plans for marriage and getting a home started, will be great and very exciting. It may be very easy to get so wrapped up in the concerns of the day, that you drift away from a close relationship with the Lord.

How do we keep these good things in life from distracting us from the best? I'm not sure I have the answer to that question. But I have some experience. It's a battle I fight every day.

I think the secret is to integrate your spiritual life into every single hour, into every single area of your life. Every decision has spiritual implications. Every decision involves the deployment of some of your time, energy, and financial resources. To maintain a correct focus, involve the Lord in every decision and commit it to Him. Open every day and close every day with a quiet conversation with Him. Converse frequently with Him during the day. By praising God, you acknowledge He is the most important influence in your life. By your requests, you acknowledge your need for Him to guide, direct, and answer your prayers.

The danger is that you leave your Christian disciplines for a time and become distracted from prayer, reading, and fellowship with other Christians. The result: Even what could be considered good things in life cause you to begin walking the way of the world — and that's a way which never totally satisfies.

I am convinced Satan clothes himself in the good things just to distract us from the best things. You need to be the best you can be in your career. But if a career demands 15 hours a day at the cost of separating you from things of the Lord, such a distraction can lead to a negative pattern of life. Satan wants to neutralize you into a Christian who can speak the truth, who knows the truth, but who basically flows with the way of the world. That life pattern, although it looks fine to most, lacks distinction and eternal impact.

The "lukewarm" Christian is common in Christianity today. Such a person is characterized by an unwillingness to sacrifice, to invest in others, to stand up for what's right, or to fight against certain Satanic tides of the times. We are distracted with so many other good things such as succeeding in a career, involvement in good social activities — and sometimes even Christian service activities — that we sever communications with God.

With the tremendous pressure of the "world system" in every medium, it's a real battle to live a life with eternal impact.

God gives each of us a spiritual "job description" that

matches our background, our spiritual gifts and personal interests. When you fulfill your appointed role, you become a unique entity with a unique purpose. By finding that spot with a local church and in the body of Christ, you are finding your highest and best use from an eternal point of view. And, you avoid the distracting "junk piles" of life by focusing on God's best.

18 Success

Get a High View

Constantly remind the people about these laws, and you yourself must think about them every day and every night so that you will be sure to obey all of them. For only then will you succeed.

(Joshua 1:8)

Have two goals: wisdom — that is, knowing and doing right — and common sense. Don't let them slip away, for they fill you with living energy, and are a feather in your cap. They keep you safe from defeat and disaster and from stumbling off the trail. With them on guard you can sleep without fear; you need not be afraid of disaster or the plots of wicked men, for the Lord is with you; He protects you.

(Proverbs 3:21-26)

The verdict was in. The tests were complete. They showed the fast-growing type of cancer. It was my duty to tell your Grandfather Oster the bad news about his health. He was resting in the family room which overlooked the farmyard where two previous generations of Oster farm families had labored.

In communicating with each other, Dad and I chose the direct approach. "Dad, the doctor's report is in, and it is not good. It's malignant, and a fast-growing type. There are some things the doctors want to do on Tuesday..."

I paused; Dad's eyes focused on mine. He simply gave me one firm, deep, understanding nod. He seemed to say, "I understand. I sort of expected it. I am ready." Although he didn't verbalize those words, our relationship over the years made the simple nod of the head speak volumes. Dad's understanding nod told me that faith works. More practical than any Sunday School lesson or sermon, Dad's simple way of accepting that the final chapter of his life was right before him deepened my faith.

In a totally calm manner, Dad indicated beyond any shadow of a doubt that his faith, placed in Christ as his Saviour nearly 25 years earlier, was the only preparation he needed for his final days. There are many definitions of success in today's world. But reaching the end of life totally prepared to make that journey to Heaven is the final proof of your relationship with Christ.

Last night you told your mom and me you could never remember your Grandfather Oster saying an unkind word. You were only five when your grandfather died, but what an impact his kindness had! Neighbors and business people all shared your memory of him. One aspect of success is living life so the memory of your caring personality lingers for years.

The doctors were correct in their diagnosis. Six months later, Dad went to be with the Lord. At the funeral home one of the truck drivers who had delivered feed to the farm for many years looked away from the casket and said simply, "Harland was a good man." That was a commonly-held opinion as family and friends from the nearby town of New Hartford, population 500, filled the Downing Avenue Gospel Chapel to overflowing. They paid their last respects to a friend taken at age 53. Somewhere in defining success you must make room for leaving the kind of legacy your grandfather left — the respect of hundreds of acquaintances he made in the farming community where he lived from birth to death.

Part of the reason your grandfather was such a large person in your life is that whenever you entered his life, you were No. 1. He dropped his work to entertain you. He took great joy in telling the story of how the two of you rode to town in his truck. You began to complain of a "headache." He stopped at the elevator and got a bottle of orange pop for you. You exclaimed, "Poppy, my headache is all better now!" Success in Dad's mind was being able to enjoy and retell family stories like your cure for the common headache.

One definition of success would be to view the world as God views it. Even without a deep understanding of theology, your grandfather had that ability — whether in the way he cared for his children and grandchildren, or the way he took care of his crops and livestock, he viewed himself as a steward. You are fortunate to be the recipient not only of Christian training from your childhood, but of the opportunity to personally view people like your grandparents who delighted in "pleasing God."

We were created to glorify the God who made us. What does God want us to do? He wants us to honor and praise Him in all we do and say. So we need to get our eyes off ourselves, and on the plan of God. The peace, joy, love and purpose in life that all of us desire are found in the pursuit of God, not in self-enhancement.

The truly successful people I know are pursuing God by using the resources He has given them in every area of life. They advance the cause of Christ in many ways in their community. Christianity becomes an every day, every hour outliving of the inliving Christ. Interest in others and service to others is a natural response. Success follows. Yet, while others strive so hard for success as an end in itself, so frequently they end up empty-handed and heavy-hearted.

One of the challenges of your life will be to constantly reflect on God's word and to maintain a correct view of true success. The world has an upside down view of success. A. W. Tozer wrote nearly thirty years ago, "This mania to succeed is a good thing perverted. The desire to fulfill the purpose for which we were created is of course a gift from God, but sin has twisted the impulse about and turned it into a selfish lust for first place and top honors. But by this lust the whole world of mankind is driven as by a demon and there is no escape.

"Excessive preoccupation with the struggle to win narrows the mind, hardens the heart, and shuts out a thousand bright visions which might be enjoyed if there were only leisure time to notice them."

19 Work Ethic

The Reward of Work Is Satisfaction

But Jesus called them together and said, "Among the heathen, kings are tyrants and each minor official lords it over those beneath him. But among you it is quite different. Anyone wanting to be a leader among you must be your servant. And if you want to be right at the top, you must serve like a slave."

(Matthew 20:25-27)

As I drive across a bridge over the Platte River near North Platte, Nebraska, the large chunks of ice breaking loose are a sure sign of winter's demise. The smoke trickling up from a single farmhouse chimney is the only sign of life I can see. A satellite receiving dish in the front yard is a symbol of a fast-changing life in rural America. An amazing drama has unfolded during the lives of the generation of agricultural businessmen who are retiring today.

Had your Grandfather Oster not been stricken with cancer at age 53, he would have been retiring about now. His generation spanned the period from horse-drawn implements to satellite receivers.

It has been 35 or 40 years since your grandpa hung

129

up the horse harness and switched totally to mechanical power. I recall, as a child on the farm, about the only thing left for horses to do was pull the corn planter. Tractors had already replaced horses on most farm jobs. But on soft ground at corn planting time, Dad preferred horses right up until the mid-1940's. There no doubt was some cost efficiency, also. I remember Dad saying in the days of gas rationing, "We can grow the fuel for these horses, but we've gotta buy gas for the tractors."

Dad started farming in early 1942 "on a shoestring." He was so close to being without cash that he occasionally had to substitute humor for his inability to buy presents for Mom's birthday. On one such occasion, with a twinkle in his eye, he told Mom her birthday present was in the barn. She knew something was up, but followed him across the road and through the horse barn door where Dad proudly showed her a new set of horse harnesses. Mom took it good naturally, but she repeated the story on subsequent birthdays with enough frequency that it became indelibly impressed on my mind. It's an interesting comment on Dad's farming career, marriage and sense of humor.

The satellite dish is not the only sign of change as I drive across the Great Plains. Abandoned farmhouses, idle acres retired by a federal farm program, empty stores on the main streets of even sizable towns — these are the scars left by the shock of going from wild inflation in the 1970's to rapid deflation in the 1980's. Changes came so fast and hard that, like a financial earthquake, they left certain farm families in financial shambles. The impact will probably forever change the face of rural America. Towns are losing their grocery stores, hardware stores and high schools.

Half-empty church pews are a sad reminder these busy rural hubs of yesteryear serve a dwindling clientele.

To remain competitive and to effectively use the machinery that's available today, one person now farms what was farmed by 20 or 30 families when your grandpa was young.

I'm not one to look back and try to hang onto the past. But I am concerned that some of the changes will wipe out certain values and institutions that have shaped America. We don't have to throw away the good things of our past as we move into the future, but that might happen if we're not careful. The disciplines learned by hard work on the farm are one possible casualty.

For example, by working on the farm with my father and mother, I had a sense of belonging and of being needed. I recall having regular chores at age six: filling up a hog watering tank every night after school. At age seven, I gathered eggs every night. At age eight, I began hauling 5-gallon buckets of feed and water into the henhouse. At age nine, I was in the full routine of farm chores every night, helping with feeding the calves, bedding down the cows after milking, washing up the milk pails, etc.

With the help of 4-H Club work, young men and women learned how to balance a feed ration by looking at a pamphlet and reading a tag on a feedbag. We could not only spot a sick calf, but we knew which pill or injection to give it, based on some "farm boy common sense" picked up through observation. By the time we were sixteen, we had learned to operate, adjust, grease, and fix every implement that moved on the farm. And, by the time we graduated from high school, we were mentally equipped to run a small farm business ourselves. That's exactly what many young men did.

The economics learned by deciding how much expensive feed you could afford to give a pig or a calf and still make a little profit formed a logical base for making decisions in every other area of life. Now, we must look for new ways to teach the work ethic and basic economics to the younger generations.

Your mom and I urged you and David to be involved with your own regular household chores, to have part-time jobs during the summer, to be involved in paper routes, and to take part in Scouting and other young people's activities that help build values. You sold clothing, stuffed envelopes, carried papers, did baby-sitting — all to help earn your way through college. You aren't afraid to work. But I'm convinced one of the reasons much of youthful America lacks the desire to work is that many young people lack the quality of these early-life experiences. They seem to lack a sense of belonging because we have done a poor job of teaching young people how to work, and how to enjoy the satisfaction of a job well done.

Fortunately, you have had the opportunity to work in and around our business and you've had lots of part-time jobs on the college campus to give you a sense of knowing how the world works. Your confidence and knowledge level are growing. You have a head start. We need to help other young people find similar experiences.

There is a second important element of society that is being washed away by the rapid-changing trends in rural America. I believe rural people are preserving one of the largest reserves of belief in the Creator. They see God in creation every day. We can't watch the geese return regularly year after year, watch the miracle of a calf being born and a mother cow taking care of it, or watch a blade of grass grow into a stalk of corn without seeing, behind all these things, a Creator.

I'm driving across Nebraska today because I just completed a Professional Farmers of America seminar called, "Farming By The Book." We encourage farmers not only to use Biblical principles in making decisions, but help them pass these values along to the next generation. And, we want to generally encourage and help hundreds of farm families who have been through such tough economic times in America.

Rural Americans are very important to the future of America. They hold firmly to the Judeo-Christian work ethic. Their rural churches teach the Gospel of salvation by grace.

I don't have to remind you that many people your age across America do not have the sense of direction in these areas that you enjoy. Part of the reason is your appreciation of God and your understanding of the role of productive work in society. Your sense of direction and your high level of confidence are the result of a strong faith. You also have enjoyed the opportunity to show yourself and others that you have real worth in the work place, family, school and in God's great plan to reach others. We must do a better job of finding mentoring opportunities for our young people, even at the junior high age. We must show them the value of work and help integrate them into the social and economic system at a much earlier age.

The "university of the barnyard" had a pretty good system for implementing these values. One of the great challenges you'll face with your children and the generations you want to influence will be in this area of teaching the Christian work ethic in a practical setting.

If we continue to fail as a society in this area, we are setting ourselves up for the socialists who are preying on the minds of Americans today. Through a philosophy called the "Christian Liberation Theology", the liberal wings of many churches are being used to support the idea that "the way to success is to demand your rights, take from the rich to give to the poor." Such was never the teaching of Jesus Christ. He taught voluntary giving. He never taught redistribution of wealth in the way that is being pushed in some American pulpits today.

I think the reason for this fresh outbreak of enthusiasm for the liberation theology and "New Age" ideology is that socialism has always been a popular message when people are hurting financially. One thing these liberal theologians are telling farmers is that "everyone in America deserves a 160-acre farm, and an economy that guarantees a living wage on that farm."

Unfortunately, this idea is finding some favor as it reaches the ears of people who have been hit hard by "whipsaws" in our economy and who seek any ray of hope for survival. Hopefully, you can help others think through the issues of work and responsibility so the empty ideas of the liberation theology movement run out of gas in your generation.

When a society replaces hard work with a government check, productivity goes down, the standard of living goes down, inflation goes up, debt goes up. You live in such a society. Maybe we can change the directions a little by personally enjoying our wok, helping others to enjoy theirs — and by seeking out candidates for political office who share our view of a limited government role in our private lives.

20 Influence

Have an Impact on Your Culture

*Stop loving this evil world and all that it offers you, for
when you love these things you show that you do not
really love God; for all these worldly things, these evil
desires — the craze for sex, the ambition to buy
everything that appeals to you, and the pride that comes
from wealth and importance — these are not from God.
They are from this evil world itself.*

(1 John 2:15-16)

When your brother, David, was in kindergarten, he
was given the privilege of taking care of his class' pet gerbil
for the weekend. Quite reluctantly, he allowed you to pet
the gerbil. A crisis occurred on Sunday afternoon when
you picked the gerbil up by its tail — and the end of the tail
fell off. I will never forget the startled expression on your
face. You looked up at David and asked, "Does God still
love me?" David's disgruntled response was, incorrectly,
"No!"

Even at age three, you had developed a concern for
right and wrong from God's point of view. That sensitive
nature amazed your mother and me. It emerged in conversations around our dinner table, and, after Sunday School
classes you attended. By living out your sense of values

135

and passing it on to the next generation, you have an impact on the culture of our entire nation. The character of our nation is an integrated, almost invisible thing that grows out of its citizens' sense of right and wrong.

Especially in the few years since you were born, America has eroded the cultural norms that have undergirded our society. Change can be healthy. But, in national morality, America is drifting hopelessly on a raft of relative, secular standards. Everyone, including Christians, will pay the cost of sexually-transmitted diseases, drug-related deaths and emotional stress and strain.

When we traveled to Australia, I saw an Australian newspaper editorial which made an important point about Japanese culture. The writer pointed out that it would be extremely difficult for other countries to copy Japan's economic success because the cultural norms that underlie Japanese society are distinctive. The editorial pointed out there is a direct relationship between culture and economic performance: "If a society has a tradition of valuing education, hard work, industrial harmony, saving money for investment, and a great respect for authority, it is likely to perform better economically than a society that does not value these traditions."

There is no reason why American culture can't adapt to the radical new challenges of the 20th and 21st centuries. Our founding fathers and generations that followed them were hard workers. They were products of a value system based upon the Judeo-Christian ethic.

This nation survived an enormous civil war and two world wars as well as other conflicts like Korea and Vietnam. We have absorbed millions of immigrants from all over the world. We are blessed with the rule of law, and even today are one of the richest nations in the world. Yet, the fact remains that we are failing to build a culture and a work force with a mental attitude that admires diligence as a primary social virtue.

The workplace values that grew out of the Christian ethic are vital to rebuild American leadership, both economic and moral. These values include hard work, saving for a rainy day, and taking care of one's own retirement. It means finding joy and satisfaction in one's life work.

Today, however, a good portion of the American work force views work as drudgery. They find joy and satisfaction in weekends and vacations and live for retirement on a government check provided by taxes on someone else.

The Apostle Paul said, "I press toward the mark of the high calling of God in Christ Jesus." I don't think it is bending the context of that Scripture to say that Paul was directing us to become everything that God wants us to be. When we become the people God wants us to be, society becomes the society that it is capable of being. Obviously, a perfect society awaits the return of the Prince of Peace. That doesn't keep us from having an impact that moves our culture in a positive way by reestablishing those values which support economic, social, political and spiritual well being.

There is a body of Biblical knowledge which, if understood and applied, will help us prevent a recurrence of the economic events of the past several years. You can help shape our culture by taking positions on these and other issues and by encouraging elected officials to consider their common sense value.

1. **Individual and state greed.** The Bible speaks out strongly against wanting what someone else has. Because so many in our society want so much more than the nation can afford, we use the power of the state to rob (tax) each other in the interest of "fair-

ness." This underlying sin of envy or covetousness is a root problem which this nation has traditionally overcome. But as the nation, individuals and corporations drown in a sea of debt, national and individual repentance is needed.

2. **Government and individual overspending.** The Bible speaks in negative terms of indebtedness. "The borrower becomes the lender's slave." Living beyond our means as a family or as a nation is a sign of greed. The Bible supports a fair currency, not one which government can, in effect, devalue each year by financing its promises with gradual inflation. By overspending and allowing the currency to deflate, the government is defrauding the people just as the kings of the Old Testament clipped the edges off metal coins.

3. **Man playing God.** Whether it be in the marketplace or in the Garden of Eden, it is forbidden. To the extent that governments attempt to interfere with the marketplace to force "fair prices," it is an attempt to "play God."

4. **Freedom.** The Bible points us to a world in which the individual makes choices, and assumes responsibility for his choices. To the extent that we try, through government programs, to make everyone economically equal, we increase their dependence on and trust in Big Government. Policies should be evaluated on the basis of whether they would move a nation toward a free market economy or toward a controlled market economy. In the controlled economy, with strong central power and authority, freedoms of all kinds are suppressed. The rhetoric we hear from educators and politicians should be judged within this

framework.

5. **Responsibility.** The Bible clearly speaks of individual responsibility. Certainly each one of us must ask, "To what extent am I responsible for my own dilemma?" It is wrong to suggest we are entirely victims of circumstances totally beyond our control and expect solutions to come from government.

6. **Dignity of man.** How can the American government lecture other nations about violations of human rights while we make abortion legal? The dignity of the unborn, as well as the poor, the homeless and the aged, is a critical issue which will shape the nation's future.

7. **Biblical charity.** Another Biblical responsibility is to care for the poor and disadvantaged. American poverty programs and farm income supports have clearly overstepped society's responsibility to the point of creating a dependence upon such programs. Biblical charity was not achieved through government, but through individuals and the church.

Let me speak to you briefly about government involvement in the rural America where our family's roots run deep. Government planning sent mixed signals, causing economic chaos in recent years. Example: Congress established price support guarantees at levels greater than the value of the crops in the 1970's. As a result, farmers produced for the government, not for the market. Enormous surpluses piled up. Prices fell farther in light of huge government supplies. Government then stepped in to correct the mess they created by offering huge income support payments to farmers.

Now think on these figures: The average net equity of

all small family farmers who gross between $100,000 and $250,000 annually — that's a small family farm — was $429,891 in 1985. By contrast, the average net equity of the American family taxpayer — who is taxed to pay these farm subsidies — is about $92,000! The question of Biblical morality can't ignore any situation where money is taken from one group of middle class Americans and is given to a wealthier group of Americans. When government plays Robin Hood in reverse, taking from the poorer people to give to the richer, government involvement has gone too far.

One of the very encouraging signs I see in America is the number of people who comment on the spiritual dimension of their lives. "We're hurting, but in our trouble we have found, or deepened, our relationship with God through Christ," is the message that comes through.

Then I see this principle blossom into peace and forgiveness. Men and women help each other. Sometimes this renewed spiritual growth happens in quiet solitude, sometimes in church groups, and sometimes in small fellowship groups which have sprung up spontaneously all over rural America in the last two or three years.

Now, there's a group starting to support the local fellowships through an organization called "Fellowship of Christian Farmers, International."

If economic crisis results in the deepening of the spiritual lives of rural Americans — and I think that's a very real result — we will lay the foundation for a revitalized agriculture that will prosper in the decades ahead. Throughout the Old Testament, there appears to be a high correlation between prosperity and personal character. We're certainly building character in the crisis of the 1980's.

We must defend the concept of human freedom as

the basis for society's legal and social foundations. Free individuals produce the economic framework for the free enterprise system. And we must never take for granted the fact that the fabric of civilization rests on honest money, honoring of contracts, freedom coupled with responsibility, individual property rights, limited government, individual and group integrity and living within our means personally and nationally.

Says George Gilder, "The limits to growth are found not in God or nature, but in failures of faith and restrictions of law: all the doom-laden extrapolations of expertise deny the infinite possibilities of creative men as they penetrate the frontiers of the darkness that is always closing in on mortal minds, and reach — in risk and worship — for the inestimable treasures of light beyond."

Free choice allowed under the free market system unleashed technological progress which drives the American system, the most effective poverty-fighting system in the world. Never have so many been fed so well by so few. That's good. But, there are still poor, hungry, underprivileged people. They provide an opportunity and a responsibility for us to do much more.

21 Future

The Long-Range View Looks Great!

I pray that your hearts will be flooded with light so that you can see something of the future he has called you to share. I want you to realize that God has been made rich because we who are Christ's have been given to him!

(Ephesians 1:18)

For I know the plans I have for you, says the Lord. They are plans for good and not for evil, to give you a future and a hope.

(Jeremiah 29:11)

The worlds of East and West are moving closer together. This trend will shape your world. I've been watching part of the drama through a Chinese family.

In 1979, I visited the rural commune of Chinese farmer Chen Sing Gen, who leads an agricultural production team in the summer and a manufacturing team in the winter. His lifestyle was extremely simple in 1979. His family shared a kitchen with other families. Their wooden living room table was simple and hand-made. The davenport was a 2-inch x 12-inch plank. One large chest held most of the family's important belongings.

On the wall references to Chairman Mao included his picture and some of the sayings from the *Little Red Book* of Mao. The walls were unpainted, the floors uncovered. The room was unheated on this 45-degree winter day.

As our delegation completed its tour of the farm and his home, Chen beckoned to me to step out onto a makeshift patio. There we could see a huge expanse of land — perhaps a thousand acres or more. With a large sweeping motion of his arm, he indicated through the interpreter that most of the great expanse of land belonged to the commune. Then, with a small twitch of his index finger, he indicated to me that a plot of approximately one acre was his. Even before the interpreter told me, I knew by the glow in his eyes that Chen was about to explain something important.

In the moments that followed, Chen's discussion became one of the most moving of my entire journalistic career. He explained that this year, for the first time in his life, he was allowed to sell the production from his own plot in small-town markets free from government control. He could price his product in competition with other "free market gardeners." As the American farm boy who grew up with the dream to own his own farm, I could really relate to my fellow Chinese farm boy.

I asked Chen how he would spend the profit from the crop. He confided that he was about to achieve a lifelong goal — owning his very own bicycle!

I related this story in *Becoming A Man of Honor*, the book I wrote to David. As a part of David's graduation present, he travelled with me to Japan and China on a Campus Crusade for Christ mission. In addition to delivering some Bibles in China, we revisited Chen some eight years after my first visit.

Upon our arrival at the commune, we were ushered into the conference room for a cup of tea while a messenger found my friend, Chen. The moment we caught each other's eyes, there was warmth that seemed to fill the room. We shook hands, hugged and began our conversation through an interpreter once again. He told me I was the first foreign visitor who had ever returned for a second visit to his commune. I gave him copies of the stories I had written for our *Pro Farmer* newsletter, some color pictures I had taken on the previous trip, and a Chinese Bible.

We were only minutes into the conversation when I asked if he had gotten that bicycle he'd wanted eight years earlier. He smiled from ear to ear, got up off his chair and beckoned toward the door.

I didn't recognize the area of his new home. Chen explained that a housing boom in the last eight years had wiped out the old housing, taken up his entire garden plot, and forced him to relocate into this spacious, more modern apartment-type facility.

I was amazed at what I saw the minute he opened the door. The barrenness of eight years earlier, was replaced with a homey warmth, much like an American apartment of the 1950s. An overstuffed chair and couch replaced the planks that we sat on eight years earlier. On the walls family pictures and decorative items replaced Mao's picture and sayings. The living room floor was covered with a nice throw rug. The wooden table was covered with a lace tablecloth.

Chen pointed out his favorite features. "Not one television, but two," he proudly exclaimed. He then walked me into the kitchen and showed me his new refrigerator. Finally, we got to a large laundry room. In it were *four* bicycles. "One for me, one for wife, one for son, one for daughter," Chen proudly exclaimed.

I asked, " What's left? What else do you need?"

"Only one thing," he said, "Air conditioner." I fully expect on my return, hopefully in the next year or two, that my friend Chen will have the air conditioner.

Chen and his army of free marketers have literally revolutionized China in the past few years. When the Chinese government unleashed the entrepreneurial spirit of the average Chinaman, productivity skyrocketed in agriculture. When China allowed factories to pay people for extra production, factory output shot up too.

Events in China in the 1980s sent a shock wave throughout the Communist world, causing centrally-planned economies everywhere to offer their people more individual incentives and economic opportunities. They call it "capitalistic communism!" But those two words are diametrically opposed at their roots. It appears to me communist governments everywhere have begun allowing freedoms which encourage the human spirit in a wonderful way. Hopefully, there may never be a return to Stalinist-type or Maoist-type communism.

At the very heart of most major social and political differences in the world are different points of view on the role of man. The communist sees man in total control of his destiny. (See the chart at the end of this chapter.) To maintain control, a ruling communist class uses big government to make the major decisions for the masses of people.

If you divide the world into basic categories — those people who believe God is supreme versus those who believe man is supreme — you get two different political expressions. A government that denies God as Creator is left with the theory of evolution as the only basis for its view of man. Therefore, the government takes a relatively low view of human life. Abortion and child-killing has been common in these countries for years. Mass murder of dissidents has been one of the ways large government has dominated its people. There is enormous lack of personal liberty. The group is valued over the individual in these centrally-controlled societies.

By contrast, you grew up in a nation whose very constitution acknowledges God is supreme. Framers of that constitution believed in a Creator, and valued human life as priceless. They believed in limited government, with decentralization of as many decisions as possible.

Government was divided into the executive, legislative and judicial branches, so tyrants couldn't emerge. State, county and local governments were independent from federal powers. Other founding principles were a stable currency made possible by minimum taxation, living within individual and government means, and a military large enough for the common defense.

One of the great concerns we must all have for the future is that a growing number of people in this country are willing to put their faith in mankind's own ability to plan his future. Their philosophy is moving this country on a "humanist" drift. They look for the government to handle more and more problems. As a result, the role of government has expanded immensely in the last 20 years.

Evolution taught as fact in the public school system paved the way for a society to gradually take a lower view of human life. Abortion, once considered unthinkable in this society, is now considered a right of any woman. Although we once had a nation that was driven by decentralized economic decisions, today nearly every industry must continually react to major government regulations that influence profitability.

The buying power of the dollar continues to drop. In effect, each generation is robbing the next generation of a larger and larger portion of its living standard.

It's interesting to see that the U.S., once the most powerful country in the world, is moving toward central planning while China, the most populous country, is moving toward more responsibility for individual entrepreneurs. Where will these trends take us?

I rewrite the answer to that question every year. Remember, my view of the future is limited to my current understanding of the world, the pace at which it is moving into the future, my knowledge of what drives people, and my current level of Scriptural understanding. In all of these areas I am a student, uncovering new truths and reapplying old ones in new ways every year. Let me share a few thoughts on the future:

A few weeks ago, when you and I were traveling with your mom in Australia on your "graduation" trip, I couldn't believe my eyes when I picked up a copy of *The Australian*, a local newspaper. A front-page news story predicted a one-world currency. Here's what it said: "Thirty years from now American, Japanese, Europeans and people in many other rich countries will probably pay for their shopping with the same currency. Prices will be quoted not in dollars, yen or Deutschemarks but in, let's say, the phoenix."

The story went on to tell why we will surrender our economic sovereignty in hopes of avoiding future stock market crashes like the one which occurred October 19, 1987.

A few weeks later, a story in *Financial World* indicated that "the movement of international capital, nations with roots in each other's capital, and communications networks...are undermining national borders and knitting the major trading partners — the U.S., Europe and Japan — into a single economy as intertwined as a mat of seaweed."

The story said the process is quickly moving beyond the control of governments and nationalistic politicians. One solution proposed in the article: " ... a common approach to taxing multinational income, a unitary tax that does not discourage repatriation of overseas profits or investment in the home economy and to bring the major nations' inflation and interest more in sync in order to establish a re-currency reserve system." In effect, a one-world economic system is proposed.

A story in the *London Economist* indicated, "Reformers in Russia and China seem to be blurring the contrasts between capitalist faith in the market and communist worship of the plan. Both Mr. Gorbachev and Mr. Deng are telling planners to pipe down so that factory managers can hear what markets are telling them."

What do you draw from this current talk in the press? It appears the world is moving toward a one-world economy, a one-world currency, a one-world government. The drift is in its early stages, but the rate of such a change could be startling to all of us in a world where money and ideas cross national borders electronically at the speed of light.

Where does all of this fit into a Christian's view of the world? There's a big gap between the future as represented by those press reports and the future which we see in Revelation 13. I am neither enough of a Bible scholar nor enough of a futurist to draw meaningful specific predictions from these trends. But an understanding of Revelation 13 begins to clarify where existing trends might end. This chapter speaks of a future that takes place, according to my understanding of Scripture, after the rapture. Very shortly after the Lord Jesus returns to take Christians home to be with Him, the world hits an historic low point.

Revelation 13 tells of a one-world government, with a dictator (a "great beast") as its leader. It appears from other Scripture that there is a one-world currency, or "mark of the beast" that is required for trade. This beast is so totally in control of the world's people that he can demand and get worldwide worship.

In this very dismal "period of tribulation" the world goes through a time of peace, followed by war, famine and plagues. It is a terrible 7-year period when the powers of Satan are allowed to rule the earth.

Now, that is a very dismal picture of the future. In that dismal day, the world will get to see for a few brief years what it's like to really live under the influence and control of Satan in total absence of God's people and His Spirit. The purpose of Satan has always been to take the place of God. Satan's program has never changed.

There are several things that we can glean from the view of the future as presented by the Bible.

1. We don't want to face it without Christ. That is motivation to get right with God. Christians won't go through the tribulation, in a world dominated by Satan, as I understand Scripture.

2. As we look around and see events that appear to be heading us toward this horrible one-world government of the future, there are reasons for Christians to be optimistic. We can be reassured that God has a plan. We can see His purposes and pieces of His plan unfold before our very eyes. This plan ends with an ultimate and total destruction of Satan, and a banishment of all of Satan's followers from God's presence for all of eternity. God's own people are with Him forever.

So, as a Christian, we see ourselves in the Book of

Revelation celebrating at the very throne of God with the four and twenty elders singing, "Worthy is the Lamb." That is the ultimate winner's circle. The end of a long struggle between the forces of God and the forces of Satan is a happy one for those who are prepared. Because we're on His side, we are winners, too.

If you base your optimism on an eternal view of God through the shed blood of His Son Jesus Christ, who wins the battle over Satan, you can be a true optimist!

Certainly the scientific advances of man are absolutely fantastic. But we cannot afford to place an ounce of our optimism in the hope that man ultimately will create important long-term solutions to such problems as war and hunger. Scripture tells us there will be ultimate peace, but that it will be ushered in by the Prince of Peace: Jesus Christ Himself, at the end of the tribulation period, will reestablish His kingdom on earth.

3. A study of the future reminds us the penalty of sin is very high. With that fact in mind, our view of the future should motivate us not only to personally get on God's side in this battle, but to recruit others to be a part of advancing the cause of Christ and His kingdom in this world in any way we can.

Our long-term view of the future becomes a total motivating force for our lives. Our view of the future provides a vision that drives us. Our view of the future provides hope.

4. Until the day of Christ's return, Christians are light in a darkened world. We are on a very important mission. There's no reason for us to be dis-

couraged when we see the futile results of lost man looking to himself to find answers in a world of problems. Because we know answers to questions with eternal implications, we have a significant role to play as history unfolds.

5. Throughout history, even while societies were being judged for disobedience to God, there were individuals and groups who led victorious lives. We have that opportunity to continue to snatch victories from the grasp of Satan even while society goes through a period of moral decline.

The end result of man's earthly existence has already been predicted. Read about it in the Book of Revelation. In short, this long struggle between Satan and God ends with God winning. Because we are His blood-bought children, we too are winners — victorious over sin, death and hell. Now that's victory in the true, big picture sense!

"When he, with a spirit of truth, has come he will guide you into all truth...and he will tell you things to come." (John 16:13)

PROBLEM: One nation under God or humanism

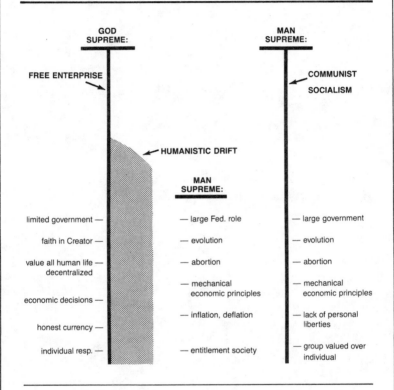

As the nation gradually drifts away from its foundation of a free enterprise system founded on a belief that God is supreme toward one where man is supreme, the system sputters under rules it was never intended to follow. Result: Spiritual bankruptcy.

This trend leaves huge implications for the nation as moral fiber decays and the continual habit of living beyond our means undermines the value of our currency and creates intermittent inflation and deflation. First, repentance is needed. We can play a role. Second, we must learn to operate in an atmosphere of intermittent inflation and deflation as free enterprise central planners try to control the economy by first heating it up, then cooling it off again.

List of Resource Books

The Holy Bible.

Blanchard, Charles A., *Getting Things from God;* Victor Books, Wheaton, Illinois, 1985.

Bright, Bill, *The Holy Spirit;* Here's Life Publishers, San Bernardino, California, 1980.

Carnegie, Dale, *How to Win Friends and Influence People;* Simon & Schuster, New York, New York, 1936.

Crouch, Andre, "Through It All"; Manna Music, Inc., Burbank, California, 1971.

Crabb, Lawrence J. Jr., *The Marriage Builder;* Zondervan Publishing Company, Grand Rapids, Michigan, 1982.

Elliott, Elizabeth, *Let Me Be a Woman;* Tyndale Publishers, Inc. Wheaton, Illinois, 1976.

Foster, Richard, *Celebration of Discipline;* Harper & Row, New York, New York, 1978.

Gilder, George, *Wealth and Poverty;* Basic Books, New York, New York, 1981.

Heavelin, Marilyn Willett, *Becoming a Woman of Honor;* Here's Life Publishers, San Bernardino, California, 1988.

Hocking, David L., *Pleasing God;* Here's Life Publishers, Inc. San Bernardino, California, 1984.

How to Use Your Money God's Way. How to Manage Your Money; Ron Blue & Co., February 1988.

Johnston, Russ, *God Can Make It Happen;* Victor Books Wheaton, Illinois, 1976.

Keller, Phillip, *Salt for Society;* Word Books, Waco, Texas, 1986.

McDowell, Josh, *The Secret of Loving;* Here's Life Publishers, Inc., San Bernardino, California, 1986.

McGinnis, Alan Loy, *Bringing Out the Best in People;* Augsburg Publishing House, Minneapolis, Minnesota, 1985.

Meredith, Don, *Becoming One;* Thomas Nelson Publishers, Nashville, Tennessee, 1976.

O'Nan, Larry, *Giving Yourself Away;* Here's Life Publishers, San Bernardino, California, 1984.

Oster, Merrill J., "Is There a Moral Obligation to Save the Family Farm?" *Christian Businessmen's View;* Iowa State University Press, Ames, Iowa, 1988.

Oster, Merrill J., *Becoming a Man of Honor;* Here's Life Publishers, San Bernardino, California, 1988.

Rice, John R., *Prayer: Asking and Receiving;* Savior of the Lord Publishers, Murfreesboro, Tennessee, 1942.

Shepard William G. and Dexter Hutchins, "There's No Trade Deficit, Sam!" *Financial World,* February 23, 1988.

Swindoll, Chuck, *For Those Who Hurt;* Milt Nomah Press, Portland, Oregon, 1977.

Tozer, A. W., *Born After Midnight;* Christian Publications, Harrisburg, Pennsylvania, 1959.

Tozer, A. W., *The Pursuit of God;* Christian Publications Inc. Harrisburg, Pennsylvania, 1982.

Tozer, A.W., *The Root of the Righteous;* Christian Publications, Harrisburg, Pennsylvania, 1979.

Unsell, Harold, *Free Enterprise, A Judeo-Christian Defense;* Wheaton, Illinois.

Wheat, Ed., MD. *Love Life;* Zondervan Publishing House, Grand Rapids, Michigan, 1972.

"How Much Money is Enough?" *U Magazine,* University Christian Fellowship. Downers Grove, Illinois. February 1988.

"Privatizing Marx," *The London Economist;* February 5, 1988.

The Australian; Sidney, Australia, January 12, 1988.